CONTENTS

Early painting of Christ and Mary in the clouds. Circa 1360

Published by Inner Light Publications
Copyright © 1963, 1982, & 2002
All Rights Reserved By Individual Authors
For reprint & foreign rights contact Box 753, New Brunswick, NJ 08903

Cover Art © Wes Crum / Book Design, Tim Swartz / Consultant, Carol Ann Rodriguez

---

UFO RESOURCE CENTER

UFOs in Art Masterpieces
THE BAPTISM OF CHRIST
Aert de Gelder

The early artists, were known to incorporate history into their works, which made them permanent historic records, that were preserved better than other ways of documentation, such as parchment. The previous image that we published had for Aert de Gelder, was muddy and difficult to discern the meaning the artist was trying to indicate. Although de Gelder was known for his style of heavy pallet and art similar to Monet, was beyond his style, and so we went searching, in hopes of finding a better representation of this work. We have found a better representation of de Gelder's work, represented by this copy of an image, below. We then searched around, and inquired about this particular work by de Gelder. We found that "The Baptism of Christ," has far greater detail than the we had ever imagined, and certainly easier to discern than the one we had received and published in a previous post concerning UFOs in classic art series. Some of those details are as follows:

NAME: The Baptism of Christ by Aert de Gelder (1645-1727) which can be found in the Fitzwilliam Museum; MEDIUM: Oil on canvas, 48.3 x 37.1 cm Perhaps c. 1710. HISTORY: This painting was given to the museum by Lord Alwym Compton, Bishop of Ely, 1905. Apparently the previous owner, named Marianne, Countess of Alford, had bequeathed it to the donor, in1888

According to our art specialist, "this particular oil painting could be found, as well as other paintings showing Jesus Christ and UFO are very presents in art until french revolution when the subject was began to be a threat for Vatican (people before this time were uneducated and were not interrested in art and paintings, except in the Renaissance time, when paintings and UFO are particularly presents) De Gelder (as Rembrandt) had access to Vatican's paintings and litterature on Jesus Christ. He had surely seen other paintings with UFOs and decided to do the same. Everyone knows that Vatican owns secret paintings and literature: all works that put the religion in dander were censured.

Other pics in arts and UFO in history can be found on this French web site :
http://marcogee.free.fr/ovni/histovni.html and

http://marcogee.free.fr/index.html

REFERENCES:

Special thanks to OVNI and Emanuel Harang for their assistance in locating this painting.

UFOS – GOD'S TRANSPORTATION?

"Lo! He comes with clouds descending," we sing lustily, with never a thought for the true meaning of the words. However, some day, and how soon remains to be seen, this will literally be true.

Of course, the "He" is the Lord Jesus Christ. The descent is the controversial second coming of the Lord. But neither of these constitutes the subject matter of my writing.

It is the clouds with which I am concerned. Not that I don't think the coming of Jesus is important -- to the contrary -- other than our Lord's first coming when He was born in Bethlehem, his second advent is probably the most important event in the history of the world.

When Jesus ascended into heaven, the Bible tells us in Acts 1:9 that "....He was taken up; and a cloud received him out of their sight." A cloud received Him. It was there ready. It could have been a dull grey vehicle, or it could have been a vapor around the vehicle. At any rate, the disciples that had gathered (over 500 of them) were told that he would come back in exactly the same way he left.

Many, many times in the Old Testament the clouds are mentioned as means of travel. For instance, Psalm 104:3, speaking of God, says "....Who maketh the clouds his chariot." Also, in the Old Testament, how about this for prophecy: Daniel 7:13,14, "I saw in the night visions, and, behold, one like the Son of man came with the clouds of heaven, and came to the Ancient of days, and they brought him near before him. And there was given unto him dominion, and glory, and a kingdom, that all people, nations, and languages, should serve him; his dominion is an everlasting dominion, which shall not pass away, and his kingdom that which shall not be destroyed."

The most remarkable cloud we read about in the Bible is the "pillar of the cloud" that went with the Children of Israel and guided them when they were brought out of Egypt. In Exodus 14:19, 20 we read of how it would change position as the circumstances warranted it. It glowed at night and made a light for the whole camp of Israel, but in the daytime it was a thick grey mass that protected them from the hot burning desert sun. In the 20th verse mentioned above, it tells us how when they were engaged in battle, or when the Egyptians drew too near the Israelites, this huge object moved between the enemy and the Israelites and would glow on the side of the Israelites, thus giving them light to perform their camp duties; while on the side of the Egyptians it was dark. When I first read that I was amazed. In my mind's eye I could see this tremendous "thing" which was necessarily <u>thin</u> in comparison to its length and width, just simply standing on end between the two camps. Not only did it aid the Israelites by giving light, while it was dark on the other side, but it stood as a shield to protect the Israelites. It was just as though God put His great big hand between them.

In Exodus, 16th chapter, when the Children of Israel had been murmuring and complaining, and Aaron had called them together to deliver a lecture on ingratitude, we are told in the 10th verse that "they looked toward the wilderness, and, behold, the glory of the Lord appeared in the cloud." So, evidently, this was some kind of vehicle that hovered over them, stood on end beside them, glowed when necessary, and put out some kind of vapor that condensed and kept a continual cloud over them to protect them from the sun (and maybe to protect the people from radiation burns), AND, somehow, God Himself was aboard.

In Exodus 19:19 we read: "And the Lord said unto Moses, Lo, I come unto thee in a thick cloud, and the people may hear when I speak with thee, and believe thee for ever." In the same chapter and the 16th verse, we read: "And it came to pass on the third day in the morning, that there were thunders and lightnings, and a thick cloud upon the mount, and the voice of the trumpet exceeding loud; so that all the people that was in the camp trembled." And no wonder they trembled. Remember, all this display of great power was preliminary to God giving Moses the wonderful Ten Commandments in person. We should tremble today when we treat so lightly that upon which God placed so great importance. Read in the 24th chapter and 15th verse how the cloud was so large it covered the top of the mountain and stayed there six days.

Well, I don't want to weary the readers with too much about clouds, but one has to start somewhere on this matter of God's transportation.

In the New Testament, Mark 14:62 says: "And Jesus said, I am; and ye shall see the Son of man sitting on the right hand of power, and coming in the clouds of heaven." Luke 21:27, "And then shall they see the Son of man coming in a cloud with power and great glory." Matthew 24:30, "....and they shall see the Son of man sitting on the right hand of power, and coming in the clouds of heaven." Revelation 1:7, "Behold, he cometh with clouds; and every eye shall see him, and they also which pierced him...."

The first letter of Paul to the Thessalonians, in the 4th chapter, beginning with the 13th verse tells about Jesus coming again for the Church. It seems that when He comes He will be accompanied by a great host from heaven. Read the thrilling words beginning with verse 16: "For the Lord himself shall descend from heaven with a shout, with the voice of the archangel, and the trump of God: and the dead in Christ shall rise first: Then we which are alive and remain shall be caught up together with them in the clouds, to meet the Lord in the air: and so shall we ever be with the Lord."

I believe that God will have provided us some kind of transportation in which to go to our eternal abode.

Well, you say, "What about the Van Allen belt of radiation? We will never make it through that!" Oh, yes, we will. In First Corinthians 15:51-52, we read:"Behold, I show you a mystery; we shall not all sleep (or die), but we shall all be changed, In a moment, in the twinkling of an eye, at the last trump: for the trumpet shall sound, and the dead shall be raised incorruptible, and we shall be changed." That means that we shall receive our glorified bodies which will be necessary to enter heaven. We are told that flesh and blood as we know it cannot enter there.

Now about this glorified body: do we read of anyone's having it before the time of Christ's advent? Of course, He possessed His glorified body after His resurrection. He was different in a way, and yet after a bit His disciples recognized Him as being their very own Lord whom they had loved so dearly. I do not want to get side-tracked from my subject, so I will not go into this.

However, in Daniel we are told of the three Hebrew children who were taken captive by Nebuchadnezzar and taken to Babylon. During their captivity there they were instructed, among other things, to positively not worship God. But Shadrach, Meshach, and Abednego continued to obey their conscience and daily worshipped God. So, Nebuchadnezzar, much against his better judgment, had them thrown into a super-heated furnace. After a bit the king himself decided to take a look to see what was happening. Imagine his amazement to see the three men walking about and enjoying themselves in the midst of the fire; and, not only that, there was a fourth one in the furnace. God had joined them, or maybe was there to greet them with His presence and a "change" for them. How else could they have withstood the heat around them except for the fact that God had changed them in a "moment, in the twinkling of an eye," and given them their glorified bodies?

So, our astronaut training will be fast, our vehicle will be ready, our Wonderful Guide will be there, and we will take such a trip as has never been contemplated because it truly staggers the imagination.

I like Billy Graham. His sermons are not so profound, but among other things he has said that impressed me is that he believed the Bible meant what it said and said what it meant; that he had decided to believe that it was God's holy word and he would stand upon it. After he made that decision, God used him mightily to win lost men and women to Himself. I, too, believe that the Bible is true, and means what it says. So many people try to "interpret" the Bible, and thereby make something dark and mysterious out of a simple statement.

In the story of the wise men of the East visiting the Baby Jesus and following the star until it came and "stood over the place where the young child was," this "star" has been explained in many different ways -- and as far as I am concerned, each of them is laughable. The favorite explanation declares the star was the conjunction of Jupiter and Saturn that occurred in 6 B.C. If so, the explanation certainly breaks down if one reads Matthew 2:9 where it says that the star came and "stood over the place where the young child was." In the first place a conjunction of planets couldn't possibly have done this. A conjunction simply means that in their orbiting, at certain times, two or more planets are so positioned that they are seen as one, thus making a very bright appearance.

In the second place, how could the wise men possibly have followed a star that was presumably in the heavens with the earth orbiting and of course changing the position of the star in relationship to the earth? Anyway, it would have been so far away it could not have possibly led the wise men even to a large city, much less to the small town of Bethlehem, and much, much less the particular stable, or cave, where Jesus was.

No, not even the wisest of the wise could have followed such a guiding star. It was bound to have been some special craft or manifestation of God that appeared to the wise men and then guided them to the very spot where Jesus could be found. Evidently this was the first time the "star" had hovered over a particular dwelling since the wise men had been following it, because we read in Matthew 2:9-11 that "When they heard the king (Herod), they departed; and, lo, the star, which they saw in the east, went before them, till it came and stood over where the young child was. When they saw the star, they rejoiced with exceeding great joy. And when they were come into the house, they saw the young child with Mary his mother, and fell down, and worshipped him: and when they had opened their treasures, they presented unto him gifts: gold, and frankincense, and myrrh."

Truly, this was an "unidentified flying object." It has never been identified, unless my ideas are correct! Why did they call it a "star"? What else would they have called a bright, glowing object that stayed above them in the atmosphere?

People will say to me, "I never saw a flying saucer." I tell them that maybe it is because they never look up.

About 1918 (I am not sure of the year), in the late summer, my whole family and I were out in the yard after an early supper. We were spending the summer down in the South Mountains where my father was born and where he had lived as a boy. We did not even have electric lights, and it was necessary to finish our evening chores early. So, we were just sitting around talking when out from behind the mountain back of the house flashed a huge, red, fiery-appearing craft that went across the sky and out of sight behind the horizon. It lighted up the atmosphere in a beautiful pink glow, and was silent as it sped across the sky. When it first appeared, my mother speculated that it was a meteor, but my father thought not because, being so low, had it been a meteor it would have fallen within our eyesight. But this sped straight across the sky and out of sight.

I was eight or nine years old at the time and remember it

Could it have been that the star that the Wise Men followed was, in actuality, a spacecraft that was sent out to announce the birth of Jesus?

vividly. At that time we didn't know much about airplanes, much less, circular, glowing vehicles.

Two years ago I was travelling west in the early evening and noticed a beautiful halo around the clouds that filled the western sky. As I watch the road pretty closely when I am driving, I did not particularly note a round, doughnut-shaped light appearing in the lower half of the clouds, until when I glanced up it appeared very bright. Upon commenting about it, my companion said, "Yes, I have been watching it for quite a time, and it glows and then fades." I immediately pulled my car over to the edge of the highway and stopped in order to observe this phenomenon better.

Surely enough, the round bright part would get brighter and brighter, glow for a moment, and then fade. This pulsating brightness was very regular. It could not have been the sun shining through the clouds because the halo and other places where the sun appeared through the clouds did not pulsate as did the doughnut-shaped part. This object was huge. However, I have seen small ones too.

I was going to work one morning early and saw a round silvery object about as big (to the eye) as a fifty-cent piece. It seemed high in the sky, but of course, I could not judge very accurately. I called several people's attention to this, and by the time I got to work, many, many people were stretching their necks and wondering what it was.

One cold night about 1:30 in the morning, my brother called me and after apologizing for awakening me in the middle of the night, said that I would forgive him when he told me what he wanted. And, indeed, I did. He told me to look to the East. Over in the eastern sky something was having itself a time. It would glow green, change to red, then amber; stand perfectly still; then dart about like crazy; never going in a curve, but always changing its course at right angles.

One Sunday about two years ago I had a telephone call from my pastor to look northwest in the sky. He is not particularly interested in flying saucers, but he knew I was, and "his people's" interests are his interests.

I ran out into the yard, and there were two rectangular-shaped objects that were colored like a rainbow. Two planes tried repeatedly to approach these two objects, but it seemed that they could come only so close, and then turn around, make a large circle and again try to approach them. The paper carried quite an article the next day, but absolutely no explanation was ever made for the beautiful, awe-inspiring objects.

It seems as if I have strayed from my subject -- but no. What I am trying to say is, that to the Christian, one who believes the Bible, space travel and UFO's, or space ships, are nothing new.

Paul says in Second Corinthians 12:4 that he "was caught up

into paradise, and heard unspeakable words, which it is not lawful (expedient) for man to utter." Whether it was beyond our comprehension, or whether he just didn't have words to describe it, or whether God told him not to tell us lest we become so homesick for our heavenly home we wouldn't be any earthly good, I don't know. Anyway, he didn't tell what he saw and heard, but he DID say he went there.

It is scriptural to watch the heavens for these phenomena. The Bible tells us that this is one of the ways we will know Jesus' return is imminent. Luke 21:27 -- "And then shall they see the Son of man coming in a cloud with power and great glory."

GENESIS

CHAPTER 1

IN the beginning God created the heaven and the earth.
2 And the earth was without form, and void; and darkness *was* upon the face of the deep. And the spirit of God moved upon the face of the waters.
3 And God said, Let there be light: and there was light.
4 And God saw the light, *t   it was good, and God divided*

14 ¶ And God said, Let there be lights in the firmament of the heaven to divide the day from the night; and let them be for signs, and for seasons, and for days, and years:
15 And let them be for lights in the firmament of the heaven to give light upon the earth: and it was so.
16 And God made two great lights; the greater light to rule the day, and the lesser light to rule the night; *he made* the stars also.

ABRAHAM'S VISITORS FROM SPACE

Flying Saucers in the Bible -- Is there any indication that they were prevalent in our earliest history? Let's give the Bible a cursory look with this in mind and see what we find. Genesis 1:1 says "In the beginning God created the heaven and the earth." The word for create here is "bara," and means to make something from nothing -- an entirely new entity. Genesis 1:2 says "And the earth was without form, and void; and darkness was upon the face of the deep. And the Spirit of God moved upon the face of the waters." The word "was" is a part of the verb "to be" and could be "the earth became without form, and void...."; or simply could be "was" meaning that at the time of which the writer is speaking, the earth was without form, and void.

"In the beginning," in the infinitely remote past, creation took place. Geologists and other scientists tell us that there is a time expanse great enough between the first and second verses of Genesis to take care of all the geologic ages of which they tell us. We do not know how many billions of years went by between the time marked off as "In the beginning" and when the Creator began to bring our wonderful Earth back into the scheme of things as a participating planet.

The word for creation that means making something from nothing is used only two more times in this chapter: Verses 21, where God made animal life, and 26, 27, where He made human life. The first

creative act, that of the heaven and the earth -- the universe --
took place in the dateless past. Something happened to it. Ages
and aeons passed, and again God's Spirit moved upon the chaos (void)
and began to call forth the light, the firmament, the waters, the
plant life, animal life, and at last, His crown of creation -- man.
With the exceptions I have noted above, all other times the word
"creation" is used in the account of creation, the word means to
call forth something that was there already.

God said a strange thing to Adam and Eve. Verse 27 says "So
God created man in his own image, in the image of God created he
him; male and female created he them." Verse 28: "And God blessed
them, and God said unto them "Be fruitful, and multiply, and replenish the earth...." Replenish. Now if words mean anything at
all, if you replenish something, it is a foregone conclusion that
it had been before; something had happened to do away with the
original supply, and it had to be REPLENISHED.

Was the earth inhabited before the creation of Adam and Eve?
We read of finding skeletons that are over a half-million years
old, and if one is bound to the theory that life began just a little over 6000 years ago, we are in quite a dilemma. I have a clip-
ping dated August 23, 1960, from The Asheville Citizen-Times, that
tells of discovering a skeleton over 600,000 years old in East Africa.

Evidently travel between the planets, or stars, or anyway, in
the universe, seemed to be a fairly casual thing. God came every
evening to walk and talk with Adam in the Garden of Eden. Also,
there were angelic beings -- and "angels" merely means "messengers"
-- and they were some kind of super-beings, or men, who came from
God to man and made God's will known to man. They would necessarily have to have some means of transportation.

The Cherubim which patrolled the Garden of Eden, and stood at
the entrance, or rather all around it, to prevent Adam from re-ent-
ering after he had disobeyed God, were evidently creatures that God
could trust. They had flame-throwers or ray guns of some kind to
guard the Garden of Eden. They evidently brought these weapons
from some other planet in space.

But before they became policemen they were very helpful to
Adam. One instance, I am sure, in which they helped Adam was in
the naming of the animal and plant life. Just think, Adam named
every bit of the flora and fauna with such accuracy as to the nature of each blade of grass and plant, and also each animal, that
the names are still very appropriate today. When one takes into
consideration the intricate names that botanists and zoologists
must remember, it simply staggers my brain to think that Adam knew
enough about the plants and animals to name them so aptly.

I wonder if after the Earth was called back into "cosmos" from
"chaos," and God created Man again, if He did not have these advanced men from other planets to help Adam. If they had visited
Earth in her previous state of fertility, they would certainly have
known about the various plants and animals.

THE MADONNA WITH SAINT GIOVANNIO

In this 15th Century painting a disk-shaped object can be seen quite clearly as it hovers in the sky above Mother Mary's shoulder. An independent witness appears in the form of a man and his dog who are looking up at the sphere. Numerous other paintings from this period contain similar scenes.

I have a time even naming my pets. I run completely out of names. It started with a dear little reddish-brown Chihuahua, whom I had named "Chippy." He in turn sired another cute little reddish-brown puppy, and as I chose him for my own, and he looked so much like Chippy, I named him "Chippy II." I couldn't think of any other appropriate name for him. Then "Chippy I" got killed by a car, and my husband got me another little -- you guessed it -- reddish-brown Chihuahua. He just had to be "Chippy III." We now have a little dachshund, and as my daughter gave him to my husband and I did not have the say-so in naming him, he turned out "Peanut" much to my grand-daughter's delight as this was her choice. He is very sweet and we love him very much.

But to leave the Frivolous and get back to the subject, let's think about Enoch, "who walked with God." He was such a godly man, and lived so close to God, that God came down often to walk and talk with him, as He had with Adam. He tried to influence the people for God, but wickedness was creeping upon them, and God told him His plans to send the great Flood upon the Earth and destroy the people. Enoch believed God to such an extent that he named his son Methuselah, which means "after me the deluge." Methuselah was the oldest man that ever lived, reaching the ripe old age of nine hundred and sixty-nine years, but he died before his daddy died, for Enoch never died! The Bible tells us in Genesis 5:24 "And Enoch walked with God: and he was not; for God took him." My idea is that one day when God and Enoch walked and talked, that Enoch wanted so much to go with God, that God just allowed him to board His space ship and off they went to the wonderful place in which God plans for us to spend eternity.

In the 6th chapter of Genesis we are told of the "sons of God" that saw the "daughters of men that they were fair; and they took them wives of all which they chose." They were bound to have been very humanoid men to marry our Earth women.

In the same passage we are told that there "were giants in the earth in those days; and also after that, when the sons of God came in unto the daughters of men, and they bare children to them, the same became mighty men which were of old, men of renown." They were superior to just ordinary people. This situation did not please God at all, but that is another story. The thing that interests me is the fact that these tremendous men came from somewhere other than Earth, and intermarried with the earth women. They were compelled to have some means of getting here!

Then turn to the Book of Job. Chronologically speaking, this book antedates Genesis. It is the oldest written manuscript we know anything about. Now Job was an actual person. Ezekiel refers to him as a model of righteousness along with Noah and Daniel (Ezekiel 14:14-20), as did James in the New Testament (James 5:11).

Satan or the Devil, was cast out of heaven, or his first estate, and was placed on Earth as a means of punishment. This happened back in the dateless past, too, and somewhere else in this book I will tell about it. However, for the present, he is dwel-

ling on Earth, but has access to space travel, because in Job 1:6
we read: "Now there was a day when the sons of God came to present
themselves before the Lord, and Satan came also among them." God
was having a conference of various space officials, and Satan was
there. But continue: "And the Lord said unto Satan, 'Whence comest thou?' Then Satan answered the Lord, and said, 'From going to
and fro in the earth, and from walking up and down in it.'"

Then God asked him about Job. The account of the trials of
Job which were brought on him by Satan, with God's permission, in
order to prove that there was at least one man on Earth who loved
and trusted God even through the most desperate situations, is a
classic.

We think we are the first generation to explore space. Maybe
so, and maybe not. In Genesis 11:1-9 is an account of what we generally refer to as the "Tower of Babel." Careful reading will reveal that this was a godless nation's attempt to probe space. God
was left out, as indeed, He is left out of the Russian's attempt
to explore space. The Russian astronaut, upon being interviewed
about his orbiting the Earth, said that he did not see any angels,
or any evidence of God out in space. Maybe his eyes were blinded
as was Elisha's servant's eyes, and he could not see what was
there. As far as that goes, I am not so sure that God is included
"in" on OUR space activities!

However, this early civilization said, "Let us" build a tower
that reaches into heaven. So God came down to see what was going
on (in a cloud?) -- and the first observation He made was "Behold,
the people is one, and they have all one language; and this they
begin to do: and now nothing will be restrained from them, which
they have imagined to do."

In other words, they were fully integrated -- economically,
politically, socially -- "the people is one." And because they had
made everything common and were so completely united in their interests, God said, "And now nothing will be restrained from them,
which they have imagined to do." If they wanted to probe space,
they could. But it seems that God wasn't ready for this to happen
at that time, and so by a very simple expedient He fixed it so they
could not communicate with each other, and therefore the work could
not go on. He confounded their language. We do have a prophecy
to the effect that during the Kingdom Age we will again have a universal language.

Prior to this, somewhere back in history, there was an attempt
made to conquer the universe -- space. Lucifer decided he wanted
to control the universe, so he attempted it. We are told in Isaiah
14:12-14: "How art thou fallen from heaven, O Lucifer, son of the
morning! How art thou cut down to the ground, which didst weaken
the nations. For thou hast said in thine heart, 'I will ascend
into heaven, I will exalt my throne above the stars of God: I will
sit also upon the mount of the congregation, in the sides of the
North: I will ascend above the heights of the clouds; I will be like
the most High.'"

"I will be like the most High." If God could go and come through the vast stretches of His universe, Lucifer wanted to do the same thing. But Lucifer destroyed himself through pride, and God cast him into the earth, where he certainly is busy today!

There is an asteroid belt that maintains an orbit around our sun that scientists speculate was originally a planet that exploded -- and maybe exploded because of atomic fission. Isn't it strange that they refer to this defunct planet as Lucifer?

In the fifteenth chapter of Genesis, we are told of how God assured Abraham that he was pleasing to Him, and that God accepted the work that Abraham was doing. God instructed Abraham just exactly how to place a sacrifice. Even down to the most minute detail as to how to arrange the offering on the altar. Abraham did as he was bid, and sat down to wait. He kept the birds of prey fought away from the sacrifice so that nothing was taken off the altar, and after dark, there Abraham stayed guarding his sacrifice. (We should be very careful never to take anything off the altar that we have placed there. So many times we promise God various things -- to tithe, to go to Church regularly, etc., and the first thing we know we have gone to sleep and forgotten that we have dedicated certain things to God, and the birds of worldiness come and steal away our good intentions.) Not so Abraham. He kept everything on the altar he had placed there, and after dark, "behold, a smoking furnace, and a burning lamp passed between those pieces" and consumed them, thus indicating that God accepted his offering. I wonder just what the "smoking furnace" and "burning lamp" was. It was evidently something very definite and material. It glowed like a red hot furnace, and was either so hot it burned up the sacrifice, or had some kind of rays that completely disintegrated the various animals on the altar.

In the eighteenth chapter of Genesis we have the strange account of the Lord Himself, accompanied by two men, visiting Abraham. Abraham was resting during the heat of the mid-day when he looked up and there were three men standing there. We know one of them was the Lord because the first verse of this chapter tells us that. The other two were visitors from outer space somewhere, because Abramah calls them angels. They had some serious business with Abraham. God was very displeased with the neighboring cities of Sodom and Gomorrah, and as Abraham's nephew, Lot, had chosen to go there to live and has raised his family in this godless place, God was going to give Abraham a chance to get Lot out, or at least to warn him.

I want you to bear in mind that these men had to have some means of transportation in order to come to Earth. Also, they were really men, because Abraham, anxious to show great hospitality to his unusual visitors, hastened into the tent and told Sarah to hurry up and make them some "cakes" out of the very best and finest meal they had, and he ran to tell a servant to dress a young tender calf as quickly as possible. Then he brought out fresh country butter and milk, and prepared a place for them under the trees where it was as cool as he could muster in the middle of the day.

But Abraham, himself, was too excited to eat (I would be, too), and stood by them under the three, "and they did eat." So they were very much men.

Now the Lord sent the two men on to Sodom to try to get Lot out before the terrible judgment should fall. The Lord stayed on with Abraham, and the story of how Abraham pleaded for the wicked city is a very touching one.

The Bible is very meticulous in what it says. The 19th chapter opens with these words: "And there came <u>two</u> angels to Sodom at even...." Lot invited them to his house and "made them a feast .....and they did eat."

We are often told in various books that the space people are very much like us, and according to the Bible, this is evidently so. Even the people of Sodom mistook them for ordinary men.

The story of the destruction of Sodom and Gomorrah reads like a story written today about the destruction of a city by an atomic bomb. In Genesis 19:24, we read: "Then the Lord rained upon Sodom and upon Gomorrah <u>brimstone</u> and fire from the Lord out of heaven." The word used here for brimstone is "goprith," and is always used in connection with judgment. In Deuteronomy 29:23 where this word is used, it adds that no grass ever grew upon the land where this particular kind of "brimstone" fell. In the Septuagint translation the same word is used all through Revelation to describe Hell.

I do not know the meaning of the atom, and the meaning of nuclear fission. I do know that in II Peter we are told of the awful time when the very elements will melt with a fervent heat and great noise, and that this fire has been reserved until the time that God chooses to use it. It could have been that His indignation was so great with the Sodomites that He loosed His special fire upon them. To this day the land will grow nothing, and the place is a waste.

EXODUS

CHAPTER 1

NOW these *are* the names of the children of Israel, which came into Egypt; every man and his household came with Jacob.

3 Is'-să-chär, Zĕ-bŭ'-lŭn, and Benjamin,
4 Dan, and Năph'-tă-lĭ, Gad, and Asher.
5 And all the souls that came out of the loins of Jacob were seventy

THE MYSTERIOUS URIM AND THUMMIM

In Exodus, the book of redemption, we find the account of the Israelites' deliverance from Egypt, and also in it are the detailed instructions for building the Tabernacle in the wilderness, which contained all the types and symbols of our redemption that was to come in the person of our Lord Jesus Christ. In Exodus we find minute details of instructions for every piece of furniture, every hanging, how they were to be embroidered, etc., and of course, the mysterious Urim and Thummim, about which we will say more later.

Flying saucers in Exodus? OH, YES!

First we have an account of the "burning bush" which has drawn much speculation. I don't know what it was, but something sent out such strong radiation or electricity, that everything was aglow around Moses, and was so strong in the vicinity of the bush that the bush itself looked as if it were afire -- but it was not consumed. Then someone spoke to Moses and told him lots of things, inter alia, that God was the "God of Abraham, God of Isaac, and the God of Jacob." This does not seem such an astounding statement upon first reading, but taken in connection with Jesus' statement in the New Testament, Matthew 22:32, "I am the God of Abraham, the God of Isaac, and the God of Jacob, God is not the God of the dead, but of the living," we find out that the speaker was telling Moses that this life is not all that is allotted to us, that there is a life after the experience we call "death," and that the same wonderful God that planned our intricate life here on Earth is still our God and that he has plans for us which will endure throughout eternity.

These speakers that came to Earth to deliver these messages to worthy people during times of crisis had to have some means of transportation to come from whatever part of the universe they came from. Some say "Heaven" -- well, even so, Heaven is a place. In fact, in the book of Revelation we are given some pretty definite statements as to life there and details of the buildings, streets, and so on. It may be a planet, or even many planets. Anyway, we have an eternity in which to find out.

Also, we are told that throughout eternity, "His servants will serve Him." I do not believe we will sit around and play harps, as some seem to think. I believe we will go about throughout the universe and help others as we have been helped. I also believe we will go about in space ships.

Then we have an account of the conversation between Moses and a "Visitor," wherein Moses protested his lack of eloquence in speech, and the Visitor told him that he could have Aaron as a helper, because Aaron was a good orator. This was before the days of the priesthood, and at this time the people had no means of direct communication with God. When the priesthood was instituted, God gave them the Urim and Thummim with which they could summon help whenever it was needed; but at this time, the Visitors gave Moses a rod with the words "And thou shalt take this rod in thine hand, wherewith thou shalt do signs."

After Adam was expelled from the Garden of Eden, and man became so wicked, he lost contact with God, and it seems that the heavenly visitations ceased. It was only as a good and wise man arose that believed man was destined for higher and greater living than the pursuit of material things on this Earth, that God could establish any kind of "rapport" or communication at all. This He did in significant instances.

In Hebrews we are told that "God, who at sundry times and in various manners spake in times past unto the fathers by the prophets, hath in these last days (this last dispensation) spoken unto us by his Son, whom he hath appointed heir of all things, by whom also he made the worlds." This is a marvelous passage of Scripture, and it goes on to tell us that not only did Christ make the world, but that He "upholds everything by the word of his power." In other words, the reason all nature works with such harmony, the reason the buds come out in the Spring, the reason the sun makes its appointed rounds, or rather the Earth, and we see the sun come up in the East every morning, is because Christ says so.

Now, we are told that God speaks to us in these last days by Jesus. During this present dispensation of time, God has not seen fit to visit us as He did back in the days of Israel's early history. When He gave us Jesus, in Him we could see God's plan for mankind -- how He intended us to live and behave. Also, Jesus told us of the life after death, and what we could expect to happen.

However, in these very "last days," it seems that we have these visitors from outer space again. Things are beginning to happen. Jesus said that just before His return (Luke 21:25) "There shall be signs in the sun, and in the moon, and in the stars,.... for the powers of heaven shall be shaken. And then shall they see the Son of man coming in a cloud with power and great glory. And when these things begin to come to pass, then look up, and lift up your heads; for your redemption draweth nigh."

Exodus, as I said before, is the book of redemption from Egypt, but it typifies our final redemption from an Earth of hardship, to an unlimited universe of wonderment and opportunity for service.

Another remarkable story in Exodus is the account of the Bethel Stone, although the story of this rock runs all through the Bible, and in fact, is still a part of history today. The first time we see it mentioned is really in Genesis, Chapter 28, where Jacob, after stealing his brother's birthright, fled. He became weary as night came on, and stopped at a certain place which he later named "Bethel." He gathered some stones to make himself a pillow, one in particular, as we shall see. He must have just leaned against it, as it turned out to be a fairly large rock.

During the night he had a dream. He dreamed of a ladder that was set up between Earth and Heaven, and angels went up and down on it. But there was a reason for the visitors. They brought Jacob the most important message the House of Israel was to receive.

God told Jacob, by messenger, no doubt, that He would give him all the land around there. The exact tract of land is given in another book of the Bible, and is of course, Palestine. However, it is not the Palestine we know today. It covers much more territory, but some day Israel will have every bit of it again. He also told Jacob (whose name was changed to Israel, Prince with God) that he would go away from that land (Palestine), but that he would surely return and possess it, and also that He, God, would be with Jacob and protect him wherever he went.

Jacob was very impressed with his "dream." Just read: "And Jacob waked out of his sleep, and he said, 'Surely the Lord is in this place; and I knew it not.' And he was afraid, and said, 'How awful (full of awe) is this place! This is none other but the house of God, and this is the gate of heaven.' And Jacob rose up early in the morning and took THE STONE that he had put for his pillow, and set it up for a PILLAR, and poured oil upon the top of it. And he called the name of that place Bethel: but the name of the city was called Luz at the first.....And this stone, which I have set for a pillar, shall be God's house: and 'of all that thou shalt give me I will surely give the tenth unto thee."

Now if there is any doubt in your mind that this was a moving experience for Jacob, just cast your doubt aside when you read that Jacob was so impressed that he promised to give a tenth of everything he would ever acquire from then on. And he did. When any experience is tremendous enough to make a man, particularly of Jacob's instincts, open his pocketbook, it is a tremendous experience indeed.

The stone stayed with the Israelites from then on. Either Jacob took it to Egypt when he went down in his old age to join his son Joseph, or Joseph took it back with him after the burial of his father. Jacob made Joseph custodian of it. Genesis 49:24: "..... the shepherd of the stone of Israel."

It is a strange story of how this same rock finally came to rest in Westminster Abbey, and how all the kings and queens of England have been crowned on this same stone.

When the time came for Queen Elizabeth II of Great Britain to be crowned, there was much consternation in England. A catastrophe had befallen the nation! The Stone of Scone, the Bethel Stone (and it went by various other names), was missing!

Probably all of you remember the many accounts and the headline news given in April, 1951, to the missing stone. Some young men from Scotland, Scottish Nationalists, had stolen the Coronation stone from Westminster Abbey on the preceding Christmas morning. Great Britain could not have its precious Coronation ceremony without this stone.

Well, finally they found it, and Queen Elizabeth was crowned with much pomp and ceremony. I remember watching it on television, and later LIFE magazine carried pictures in color of the Coronation. I watched with great interest as Queen Elizabeth would move about from throne to throne, dragging her ermine and expensive gown and train, but when the propitious moment came for the crown to actually be placed on her head, it was on the rather plain board seat that contained the rough old sandstone rock, that the Coronation actually took place.

This is supposed to be the very same stone that was carried by the Children of Israel from Egypt, through their desert wanderings, and finally into Palestine, which was the land of promise. How it left there and finally turned up in England as the Coronation Stone is an exciting story.

As mentioned before, either Jacob or Joseph took the Stone to Egypt, and since Jacob in his dying bequest made Joseph custodian of it, the Stone of Israel would be kept by Joseph's posterity.

When Israel left Egypt in the great exodus, the Stone went too. Paul refers to this fact and likens the stone to Christ in First Corinthians 10:1-4.

It was the Rock from which they got water during their wanderings. Moses gave two accounts of this; one in Exodus 17:6, where it occurred at Rephidim near Horeb; and in Numbers 20:9-11, many miles North at Kadesh near the desert of Zin.

Joshua records the fact that this stone "heard all the words" of the Israelites and would be used as a witness either for or against them. What if they should be reproduced?

The Stone is referred to several times as an emblem of Christ, Isaih 28:16-17, being one such mention.

Zechariah tells us it shall be brought forth at the greatest Coronation yet: Zechariah 4:7.

This Stone was kept in the Temple during Israel's flourishing years, but what became of it when the Temple was destroyed and Judah was taken captive to Babylon? One would think that the emblem for God's earthly Chosen people would be something priceless, such as a huge diamond -- but no -- it was simply a Stone, but they treasured it above all they had with the exception of a few other articles. The Ark of the Covenant with its contents ranked in value with the Stone of Destiny.

Ezekiel addressed a message to Zedekiah (the last king of Judah) in Ezekiel 21: 26-27, in which he prophesied that the kingdom would be overturned three times, or "turned aside." Things looked dark, but read Jeremiah 33:17, "For thus saith the Lord; David shall never want a man to sit upon the throne of the house of Israel." Well, in view of what happened to Zedekiah soon after that, things looked pretty hopeless, because the throne ceased in Palestine when Zedekiah was taken captive to Babylon -- but God promised that there would always be a ruler of the house of David ruling over the house of Israel. Remember, that at this time, Judah and Israel were two different kingdoms.

Ten-tribed Israel was carried captive into Assyria 130 years before Judah was taken to Babylon. They went from Assyria through the gate of the Caucasus Mountains by one of the passes known as the "Israel Pass" (II Esdras 13:41-45). (Note: Esdras is an Apocryphal book of the Bible).

Just prior to the destruction of the City and the Temple, God had Jeremiah purchase a plot of ground at Anathoth (Jeremiah 32:7-

15) and had him hide the Stone there. About this time, Zedekiah fled by night and his sons with him, but was overtaken on the plains of Jericho, and he and his sons were taken captive to Ribleh in the land of Hamath, where his sons were slain and Zedekiah's eyes were put out. Then he was taken to Babylon where he died (Jeremiah 39: 4-7). However, the king's daughters were spared. In Numbers 26:33 we have the statement that "Zelophehad the son of Hepher had no sons, but daughters," and gives the names of his daughters. In the 27th chapter we have an account of how these girls came to the ruling body of Israel after their father's death and requested that a law be passed in Israel that a man's inheritance could pass to his daughters, if he had no sons. This seemed fair, and the law was passed. Heretofore, women had no rights of inheritance.

But Jeremiah remembered God's promise to keep the line of David, the royal house, alive, and in Jeremiah 43:6-7, he gives an account of how he took the Kings' daughters, and a few others that Nebuchadnezzar's men had overlooked at the palace, and Baruch the scribe, and fled to Egypt. God never wanted any of His people in Egypt, and hadn't changed His mind at this stage of the game, and they went to Egypt against His will, but they did not stay long, but left. In Jeremiah 44:28 we have the record of how they escaped.

Remember Jeremiah had a special mission in life (Jeremiah 1: 10), among other things he was "to plant." God assured Jeremiah that his and Baruch's life would be safe until his mission was performed, and that he would bring them into some unknown far-off land (Jeremiah 15:11-14).

There is no further record in the Bible of what happened to Jeremiah, Baruch, or the King's daughters. But the Prophet Ezekiel, in the form of a riddle and parable to the House of Israel, shows the removal of Zedekiah, and the planting of a royal Princess in some land other than Palestine, as Palestine was to become a desolation. Ezekiel 17:22-23: In this passage where it says, "I will crop off from the top of his young twigs a tender one, and will plant it upon a high mountain....," the words "tender one" is Tea Tephi, of which I will say more later.

The signs of Jeremiah in Egypt are his own writings and the testimony of the Jews, corroborated by E. Flinders Petrie, who in 1887 discovered the "Palace of the Jew's Daughter" at Taphanhes, Egypt. Jeremiah disappeared from sight with the escaping remnant. That he visited Palestine to complete his work and gather certain relics is clear from the record of things he had when he arrived in that far country.

Following the disappearance of Jeremiah from Egypt, there appears in Western history a man with a group of people who answers in every respect to the description of Jeremiah, who had with them certain valuable relics. The evidence of all this is voluminous from Irish history -- for that is where Jeremiah went -- to Ireland.

A few of the recorded facts are:

Tea Tephi (Tender Twig) is a princess from the East coming to Ireland at this time. She was known as the King's Daughter, and her guardian was the Prophet Ollam Folla, which means "Wonderful Seer." They had a chest with them which contained:

The Urim and Thummim breastplate (Exodus 28:30)

Lia Fail (The Bethel stone, Stone of Destiny, and many other names. Lia Fail was the Irish name for it.)

David's Harp ("The Harp that Hung in Tara's Halls")

Ark of the Covenant (some evidence)

The story of the coming of the beautiful princess to Ireland has been told in song and poetry for many years. Here is a poem from "The Irish Chronicles" that records the fact of the coming of the Eastern princess. This poem purports to set forth the facts as told by this Princess:

"We were five that rode on asses,

And five by the mules they led
Whereon were the things brought forth
From the House of God when we fled;
The Stone of Jacob our father,
The seat wherein Yahveh dwells
Upon Sacred things whereof the Book of
the Prophets tells.
And the signs of my father David,
On whom was the promise stayed
Bright as the crown of the dawn,
Deep as the midnight shade.

* * *

Upon me was that promise fallen.
For me was the Prophet's toil.
He had signed me with David's signet,
Annointed my head with oil.
He had set my hands to the Harp;
He had bidden me hold the spear (scepter);
The buckler was girt to my bosom,
And Barach and he drew near
To set my feet upon Bethel,
The stone that is seen this day.
That my seed may rest upon it
Where'er it is borne away:
And its promises be sure beneath them,
Strong to uphold their throne;
Though the builders cast it aside,
It shall never be left alone."

The altars of ancient Ireland were called Botal, or Bothel, meaning House of God. That is, it is the Hebrew word B-th-l (no vowels) and has the same meaning. Hence, if this coronation stone which is in Westminster, which the English call Jacob's Pillow, and which their Scotch and Irish ancestors call "God's House," or "B-th-l," the "Stone of Destiny," is indeed what its name and history declare it to be, then it is the very throne of David upon which the sons of David were formerly crowned in the Temple of God at Jerusalem. How about the English kings and queens that are presently crowned on it? Well, I'm certainly not going into that -- it is too controversial, being what is generally known as the "British Israel" theory.

Some of the names applied to this stone are very interesting. To the Hebrews it was the

> Precious Stone
>
> Stone of Majesty
>
> The Chief Corner Stone
>
> Foundation Stone
>
> Stone Wonderful
>
> Pillar of Witness
>
> The Testimony
>
> The House of God.

Later, it received other names by the Irish and Scotch:

> Lia Fail (Stone of Fate)
>
> The Stone of Destiny
>
> Stone of Scone
>
> Coronation Stone.

Amerigin, chief bard to King Dermod (monarch of Ireland in the 6th century), in the notes of the ANNALS OF FOUR MASTERS, refers to the Tea Tephi as follows: "A rampart was raised around her house, for Teah, the daughter of Lughaidh (Lug-Celtic for "God," Aidh - "house"), she was buried outside in her mound, and from her it was named Tea-mur."

Queen Elizabeth II, now on the throne of Great Britain, is in line of descendants from Teah and Eochaidh the Heremonn, and in the coronation ceremony was crowned upon the "Rock."

In 1328 A.D., the Queen Mother of Edward III surrendered the Regalia of Scotland, and the Londoners allowed all the rubies, diamonds, pearls and all the coronation gear to depart for Scotland without a murmur -- but the ragged old stone -- NEVER.

On page 316, in his OUTLINE OF UNIVERSAL HISTORY, George Park Fisher (1885) has this to say:

"Edward (Edward I of England) carried off from Scone the stone on which the Scottish kings had always been crowned. It is now in Westminster Abbey, under the coronation chair of the sovereign of Great Britain. There is a legend, that on this same stone the patriarch Jacob laid his head when he beheld angels ascending and descending at Bethel. Where that stone was, it was believed that Scottish kings would reign. This was held to be verified when English kings of Scottish descent inherited the crown."

Again, in Exodus, we have an account of a momentous happening, the giving of the Ten Commandments.

The Israelites had become so unruly that Moses was unable to keep them in order. They couldn't understand how Moses and Aaron had such power and were authorized to be their leaders, when they were merely "followers." So they became "murmurers" and "complainers."

So on his next visit up on the mountain of Sinai where he talked with God, he told God about the situation. Of course, God knew anyway, but now that Moses was perturbed, it was time to act. So God told Moses, "Lo, I come unto thee in a thick cloud, that the people may hear when I speak with thee, and believe thee for ever."

Moses had seen this "cloud" many times privately, but now he was to have some witnesses -- not only of the vehicle, but witnesses to the fact that the occupants of the vehicle had a voice, and could and did converse with Moses. The people heard the voice speak in articulate words, but Moses was allowed a face-to-face audience.

We are given the reason for God's refusing to let the people see him in Deuteronomy 4:15-16: "Take ye therefore good heed unto yourselves; for ye saw no manner of similitude on the day that the Lord spake unto you in Horeb out of the midst of the fire: Lest ye corrupt yourselves, and make you a graven image, the similitude of any figure, the likeness of male or female."

In the 19th Chapter of Exodus we have all the instructions God gave Moses for preparing for this visit of the spaceship. No wonder they don't just come and visit us anytime. The terrifying conditions accompanying this particular visit was enough to convince any reasonable person that these spaceships cannot land casually.

God told Moses that he would bring his vehicle down three days from then, but first certain preparations had to be made: "And be ready against the third day: for the third day the Lord will come down in the sight of all the people upon Mount Sinai. And thou shalt set bounds unto the people round about, saying 'Take heed to yourselves, that ye go not up into the mount, or touch the border of it; whosoever toucheth the mount shall be surely put to death: there shall not a hand touch it .... whether it be beast or man, it shall not live: when the trumpet soundeth long, they shall come up to the mount .... And it came to pass on the third day in the morning, that there were thunderings and lightnings, AND A THICK CLOUD UPON THE MOUNT, and the voice of the trumpet exceeding loud; so that all the people that was in the camp trembled." And no wonder!

I don't understand about electro-magnetic vibrations, or maybe they aren't even called that, but I do know that when that UFO with its vapor-cloud surrounding it touched down upon Mount Sinai, it was a tremendous thing. Read one account: "And Mount Sinai was altogether in a smoke, because the Lord descended upon it in _fire_ (which indicates that it was a brightly glowing conveyance before it was surrounded by the cloud) and the smoke thereof ascended as the smoke of a furnace, and the whole mount quaked greatly."

The reason God didn't want the people to come too near the conveyance, or even touch the mountain over which it hovered, was because He wanted to protect them. The beams, or radiations, or whatever they were, from the spaceship, would have killed the people had they come too close.

No wonder the space people do not land their vehicles today. With our great curiosity, we would rush right up to such an object, or at least try to, and get killed for our efforts. Then the space people would be blamed for being "hostile" and killing our people.

In the midst of this very dramatic setting, God gave Moses, or rather mankind, what we know as the Ten Commandments. Moses was the greatest statesman that ever lived and he is credited with the Ten Commandments, but they were written on two tablets of stone, and evidently were prepared extraterrestrially, because the Bible says they were written by the "finger of God." So, the messengers had the Commandments all ready to hand to Moses. _They_, the tablets, were certainly very real and material, and I believe they were brought to Earth in a very real and material spaceship. They must have been very important to God for Him to take all this trouble to make them known to us. Really, the importance of the Ten Commandments is for MAN. If we would live by them as God intended for us to, what a different world this would be!

Then the Israelites were instructed to build a Tabernacle, which they did according to the most detailed instructions given to them, because everything that appeared in the Tabernacle was highly significant.

After this, God told them to establish the priesthood. Aaron was the first high priest, and to him was given the keeping of the objects known as the Urim and Thummim.

Urim and Thummim -- Lights and perfections, or lights and truth. In reading Albert K. Bender's book, "FLYING SAUCERS AND THE THREE MEN" (Saucerian Books, 1952), about his reasons for closing

MOSES COMMUNICATED WITH GOD ON MOUNT SINAI

his saucer research organization and the visits from the three men
in black, the thing that impressed me most was the small disc, or
crystal, or whatever it was the three men gave Bender with instructions that he was to use it to summon them, or to communicate
with them. With this in hand he could communicate with them telepathically. On page 91 of the book we have these words: "....We
will leave with you a small piece of metal similar to your coins.
It is to be kept in a secret place of your own.....I was to keep
the piece of metal and when I wished to make contact with them I
should hold it tightly in my palm and close my eyes, at the same
time repeating 'Kazik,' and turn on my radio. I should contact
them in two days, at this same time." On page 92, "The metal was
most peculiar. It seemed to shine almost like a light." When he
thought of showing it to someone to prove his strange experiences,
the disc glowed red and became hot.

These are strange words, and if true, stranger doings. However, we swallow "hook, line, and sinker" much stranger things as
every day occurrences. You think not? Television, for instance.
I certainly do not understand television. How in the world I can
pick up a program originating in New York or Hollywood, and not
only pick it up, but maintain just that particular program, and in
color too, is something I cannot understand. Think of the millions
of words floating around through the ether at the time your particular program is on -- how can one be segregated from all the
rest and be reproduced on my television screen? This is something
wonderful indeed.

Back in Bible times the people had not progressed to the place
where they had television, but God arranged for them to communicate
with Him, and He would answer back in a way that was unmistakable
to them. Of course, they prayed, and God answered, but that is not
what I speak of here.

The Urim and Thummim. This is a subject that is practically
never mentioned -- and I think I know why. Nobody understands it.
In Exodus 28, we have an account of how the priests were to make
their garments, and in particular, the ephod they were to wear upon
their breasts. The ephod has twelve precious stones set in it that
corresponded with the twelve tribes of Israel. They were given
careful instructions about making this ephod, and how it was to be
attached to a girdle with rings of gold and blue lace, and even the
Bible calls it "curious": "....that it may be above the curious
girdle of the ephod, and that the breastplate be not loosed from
the ephod. And Aaron shall bear the names of the children of Israel in the breastplate of judgment upon his heart, when he goeth
in unto the holy place, for a memorial before the Lord continually.
And THOU SHALT PUT IN THE BREASTPLATE THE URIM AND THUMMIM: and
they shall be upon Aaron's heart, when he goeth in before the Lord:
and Aaron shall bear the judgment of the children of Israel upon
his heart before the Lord continually." The receptacle for the
Urim and Thummim was probably a fold, or pocket, in the ephod.

Aaron was the first high priest, and again we have relationship to God being the determining factor for responsibility or

privilege with God. <u>Only the high priest could wear this peculiar piece of metal or jewel</u>, or whatever it was, and consulted it only in the holy place when some momentous decision was to be made regarding the nation of Israel. The high priest would go into the holy place alone with his Urim and Thummim and would come out with a detailed answer.

The priestly tribe was Levi. The Bible tells us a very beautiful thing about this tribe. They could not inherit land, or for that matter, could not own anything of value. The reason was that "The Lord is their portion." As Jacob had twelve sons, and we refer to the "twelve tribes of Israel," this just leaves eleven tribes to be numbered in the matter of apportioning the land, or voting, etc. But the two sons of Joseph were numbered in Joseph's place, Ephraim and Manesseh. Therefore, there were really thirteen tribes, but the tribe of Levi was special and set aside for the wonderful job of interceding with God for the people.

When Moses was old and he knew his time was short, he called all the tribes before him and blessed them. The 33rd Chapter of Deuteronomy gives this beautiful blessing and prophecy, for that it was. Each blessing constitutes the characteristics of the particular tribe receiving it, and also predicts its ultimate destiny.

As I pointed out, the tribe of Levi could not own land, but just listen to what did constitute their inheritance: (Verse 8): "And of Levi he said, Let thy Thummim and Urim be with thy holy one, whom thou didst prove at Massah, and with whom thou didst strive at the waters of Meribah...." Their inheritance was the wonderful Urim and Thummim.

When one high priest passed away, and another was consecrated in his place, quite a ceremony took place, climaxed by putting the Urim and Thummim in its place in the ephod. Read Leviticus 8:7-8: "And he put upon him the coat, and girded him with the girdle, and clothed him with the robe, and put the ephod upon him, and he girded him with the curious girdle of the ephod, and bound it unto him therewith. And he put the breastplate upon him: also he put in the breastplate the Urim and Thummim."

When a problem arose that called for the good judgment of the high priest, which was, of course, considered to be the mind of God on a matter, and the high priest went into the holy place with the Urim and Thummim, many explanations have been given by Bible scholars as to just what happened. Some say the various jewels would glow and spell out the answer in the particular matter with which the priest was concerned; or that while holding the Urim and Thummin the priest would pray and whatever came into his mind was the answer from God. I do not think this was the case. The fact that ONLY the high priest could use this object, and then only in the holy place, held some significance. I believe that in the seclusion of the holy place, God communed with the high priest. How? Did the Urim and Thummim summon someone from space to talk with the priest? When anyone else tried to use it, the result was failure. In First Samuel 28:6, we have an account of Saul, the first king of Israel, trying, but God did not answer: "And when Saul inquired of the Lord, the Lord answereth him not, neither by dreams, nor by Urim, nor by prophets."

After the exile when the people of Israel had no priesthood, the Urim and Thummim disappeared, and we never hear of it again. It is not mentioned after David's time.

But God never takes something away from us that He does not replace with something better. When He did away with the Urim and Thummim, which at best was certainly limited, he gave us Jesus, Who is universal and abounding to each and all of us. He is our great High Priest, and in Him, each of us can be a priest unto God as we stand between ungodly people and a just God. Jesus completely fulfills all the types and symbols of the Old Testament.

Note:

"God, who at sundry times and in divers manners spake in time past unto the fathers by the prophets, hath in these last days spoken unto us by his Son (Hebrews 1:1-2)."

"When he, the Spirit of truth, is come, he will guide you into all truth (John 16:13)."

"Christ is not entered into the holy places made by hands, which are the figures of the true; but into heaven itself, now to appear in the presence of God for us (Hebrews 9:24)."

When the Tabernacle was finished, and God had instituted the form of worship that was the sacrifice, and after the priesthood had been established, and it was all in working order, notice what happened: "So Moses finished the work. Then a cloud covered the tent of the congregation and the glory of the Lord filled the tabernacle. And Moses was not able to enter into the tent of the congregation, because the cloud abode thereon, and the glory of the Lord filled the tabernacle. And when the cloud was taken up (it didn't just drift away) from over the tabernacle, the children of Israel went onward in all their journeys: But if the cloud were not taken up, then they journeyed not till the day that it was taken up. For the cloud of the Lord was upon the tabernacle by day, and fire was on it by night, in the sight of all the house of Israel, throughout all their journeys." This couldn't possibly have just been clouds as we know them. It was grey by day, or maybe white, but it looked like fire at night, and every Israelite witnessed this thing. It was really in command of the Israelites' pilgrimage, because if it hovered and stayed still, they did. If it moved, they did.

Come to think of it, the Urim and Thummim could have been some kind of radio that contacted the spaceship hovering over the tabernacle.

Also, in Numbers 9:15-23, we are given a resume of this very

same phenomenon. It is worth reading: "And on the day that the
tabernacle was reared up the cloud covered the tabernacle, namely,
the tent of the testimony: and at even there was upon the tabernacle as it were the appearance of fire, until the morning. So it
was alway: the cloud covered it by day, and the appearance of fire
by night. And when the cloud was taken up from the tabernacle,
then after that the children of Israel journeyed: and in the place
where the cloud abode, there the children of Israel pitched their
tents. At the commandment of the Lord the children of Israel journeyed, and at the commandment of the Lord they pitched: as long
as the cloud abode upon the tabernacle they rested in their tents.
And when the cloud tarried long upon the tabernacle many days,
then the children of Israel kept the charge of the Lord, and journeyed not. And so it was, when the cloud was a few days upon the
tabernacle; according to the commandment of the Lord they abode in
their tents, and according to the commandment of the Lord they
journeyed. And so it was, when the cloud abode from even unto the
morning, and that the cloud was taken up in the morning, then they
journeyed: whether it was by day or by night that the cloud was
taken up, they journeyed. Or whether it were two days, or a month,
or a year, that the cloud tarried upon the tabernacle, remaining
thereon, the children of Israel abode in their tents, and journeyed not: but when it was taken up, they journeyed."

Now this was certainly no ordinary cloud. You just can't
see clouds at night, but this one could be seen -- it GLOWED at
night. We are told in another place how it gave light for the Israelites to see to go about their duties at night. I discussed
this particular "cloud" earlier in this book.

We are told in the New Testament that what this Shekinah
glory of God was to the tabernacle, and later to the temple, that
the Holy Spirit is to the Church, and to the temple which is the
believer's body. The Christian has a glow and a radiance that the
non-Christian lacks. However, I do not mean to spiritualize the
"cloud" that guided and protected the Israelites. It was very real.
And it had occupants, who often talked with Moses during these
desert wanderings, and advised him as to the best course to pursue.

STRANGE FIRE

The tenth chapter of Leviticus gives the strange account
of two of Aaron's sons, Nadab, the oldest, and Abihu.
These two men had been granted the very special privilege,
along with Moses and Aaron, of approaching the spaceship
manned by the heavenly visitors on Mount Sinai (See Exodus 24:1). In those days, as now, a little knowledge was a dangerous thing. I don't know what kind of propellant was used in the
spaceship, but suffice it to say it was powerful.

These two young men were curious, as are all young men, and
the sight of that wonderful vehicle was more than they could stand.
They evidently learned something about it, and never forgot it. But
they didn't learn everything. They knew that their father, the
high priest, Aaron, entered into the Holy of Holies once a year,
and there in the extreme privacy, for there were no windows or op-

enings of any kind except the entrance through which the high priest went, and they knew that something of great significance took place in there.

They had seen the fire of God come down upon the altar and consume the sacrifice as a token of God's approval of their obedience. So, they decided that they could split an atom themselves, and they concocted some formula for nuclear fission and the Bible tells us that they "took either of them his censer, and put fire therein, and put incense thereon, and offered STRANGE FIRE before the Lord, which he commanded them not." Whether they had the right formula, but were acting in disobedience, or whether they lacked the correct formula for the "fire," I do not know. But I do know that what they did was wrong, and their "strange fire" boomeranged upon them: "And there went out fire from the Lord, and devoured them, and they died before the Lord." Aaron "held his peace." He did not open his mouth against the punishment meted out to his sons. He knew they were wrong, and that they were tampering with something they had no business tampering with. A little knowledge is a dangerous thing.

In the book of Numbers we have an account of another visitation from space. In Chapter 12 we have the statement that Miriam and Aaron (Moses' sister and brother) had criticized Moses adversely for marrying an Ethiopian woman after his wife, Zipporah, died. It wasn't so much the second wife that bothered them as it was the fact that Moses was the leader in every way, and they were jealous.

Now Moses was very precious to God, and God took up for him when this trouble arose. Let us read: "(And the man Moses was very meek, above all the men which were upon the face of the earth.) And the Lord suddenly spake unto Moses, and unto Aaron, and Unto Miriam, 'Come out ye three unto the tabernacle of the congregation.' And they three came out. And the Lord came down in THE PILLAR of the cloud, and stood in the door of the tabernacle, and called Aaron and Miriam: and they both came forth." Then he really gave them a lecture about talking about Moses, and said he (Moses) was the one man he could talk with face to face, and then, ".....He departed. And the cloud departed from off the tabernacle."

In short, the spaceship hovered above the tabernacle, the Messenger got out, stood in the door of the tabernacle, and really gave Aaron and Miriam trouble. Then "he departed," and after he left their line of vision, the cloud departed from over the tabernacle. Anyone with any reason at all could deduce that he got into the "cloud" and it took him away.

Closely akin to the account of Nadab and Abihu, the two sons of Aaron who offered strange fire on the altar, is the story of Korah and two hundred and fifty followers, who also tampered with something they didn't know enough about. Korah was of the priestly tribe, Levi. He was jealous of Aaron and Moses, and felt that he should have as much to say about the affairs of the Israelites as Moses and Aaron. So he got him a small following, and they prepared them some of this "strange fire" and put it in their censers,

THEY TRIED TO CONSTRUCT A TOWER THAT WOULD REACH HEAVEN

and accosted Moses and Aaron with their rebellion. Now Moses knew they were treading on dangerous ground, so he went down to the place of their encampment (they were positioned next to the tribe of Reuben, who was the oldest of the twelve sons of Jacob) and warned the people to get out. Most of them did, but the two hundred and fifty that had an axe to grind stayed there, to their sorrow.

Korah had two close associates, Dathan and Abiram, and they held their ground and would not leave. The Bible tells us that God did a new thing here. He opened up the earth and swallowed them up. "And it came to pass, as he had made an end of speaking all these words, that the ground clave asunder that was under them: and the earth opened her mouth, and swallowed them up, and their houses, and all the men that appertained unto Korah, and all their goods. They, and all that appertained to them, went down alive into the pit, and the earth closed upon them: and they perished from among the congregation. And all Israel that were round about them fled at the cry of them: for they said, 'Lest the earth swallow us up also.' And there came out a fire from the Lord, and consumed the two hundred and fifty men that offered incense."

DEUTERONOMY

CHAPTER 1

THESE *be* the words which Moses spake unto all Israel on this side Jordan in the wilderness, in the plain over against the Red *sea*, between Paran, and Tŏ'-phĕl, and La-ban, and Hă-zē'-rŏth, and Dĭ'-ză-hăb.

2 (*There* ... eleven ...

and in the vale, and in the south, and by the sea side, to the land of the Că'-nă-ăn-ites, and unto Leba-non, unto the great river, the river Eû-phrā'-tĕs.

8 Behold, I have set the land before you: go in and possess the land which the LORD sware unto fathers...

MYSTERY OF THE GREAT SEAL

During their wanderings in the desert in an effort to reach the Promised Land, the Israelites came to a section of the land named Seir, which really was a mountain that just rose up out of the desert. It is southeast of the Jordan valley. In the midst of this section of the desert is what is probably the most unique and interesting place on Earth. Petra is its modern-day name. Its Old Testament name was Sela. It is a real mystery. Who established this mighty rock fortress? Who carved all the mammoth palaces in the side of the granite, or rather beautiful marble, cliff sides? And, in particular, WHO carved an eagle, just as we know the American eagle today, upon the side of the cliff?

Let's explore just a little. The second chapter of Deu-teronomy is an account of the first time the Israelites saw Petra. We also have an account in the Bible of the last time they will see it. This account is found in the book of Revelation, Chapter 12. This chapter tells of a woman (Israel) travailing in labor to bring forth a child (the Church) -- for "salvation is of the Jews, whether we like it or not, and I quote: "....and the dragon stood before the woman which was ready to be delivered, for to devour her child as soon as it was born. And she brought forth a man child,

who was to rule all nations with a rod of iron: and her child was
caught up unto God, and to his throne. And the woman fled into the
wilderness, where she hath a place prepared of God, that they should
feed her there a thousand two hundred and threescore days.....And
to the woman were given two wings of a great eagle, that she might
fly into the wilderness, into her place, where she is nourished for
a time, and times, and half a time, from the face of the serpent."

This is Petra, so I won't go into the many reasons and
proofs concerning this Scripture as why the "man child" was the
Church and not Christ, as some people think. For one thing the
word in the original for "man" is a neuter word, and does not mean
either male or female, but is a word like our word "child" and could
be either. Also, Christ was not caught up to heaven as soon as He
was born, but the Church WILL BE RAPTURED as soon as she is complete.
This is a great incentive for soul-winning. As soon as the last
person is won that can be won, Christ will come for His bride.

But as I say, this is about Petra, so let's go back. Abraham had two sons, Isaac and Ishmael. Ishmael became the father of
the Arabs. Isaac became the father of Jacob and Esau. Jacob,
whose name was changed to Israel, became the father of the twelve
boys who headed the twelve tribes of Israel. Esau became the pro-
genitor of the Edomites. These Edomites were bitter enemies of the
Hebrews, or Israelites, and the Old Testament is full of accounts
of wars between them. Saul fought against the Edomites (I Samuel
14:47); David subdued them, and from their rich mines took gold
and silver for the temple at Jerusalem (II Samuel 8:14 and I Chronicles 18:11-13). Solomon ruled them at one time (I Kings 11:1-22).

Then we have the strange account of Hadad, who was taken
to Egypt as a child, and held captive there until he was a young
man. When he found out that David was dead, he asked permission
to return to Sela, or Petra, and was granted this favor. This
probably accounts for the appearance in Petra of the two Egyptian
obelisks that stand sentinel in Petra. The whole top of a hill
was carved down and left these two rose-red marble obelisks standing there.

Eventually, the Edomites were driven out of Seir, and the
Arabs took over and made Petra their capital. For centuries Petra
was a rich caravan city crossroads of the ancient world. The Ara-
bian Peninsula was a network of caravan routes over which passed
products of Africa, Arabia and India to the valley of the Nile,
Palestine, Phoenicia, and the Euphrates-Tigris valley. For nearly
a thousand years (6th Century B.C.) goods were brought to Petra for
storage and transshipment. The Romans built two roads to tap its
wealth. When Rome fell its doom was sealed.

For more than a thousand years, Petra was lost to the
world. It became abandoned, and its almost impossible approach was
forgotten, until in 1812, John Lewis Burckhardt (a Swiss) discovered
it, and after World War I, a few travelers began to go there to view
it.

At that time it took a month to travel from Jerusalem to
Petra by caravan trail. But soon the Mecca railway from Damascus
to the Sacred City Medina was built. It went through Ma'an, which
is the closest point to Petra. Later a highway from Jerusalem to
Ma'an was built, with a dirt road from Ma'an to Eljii, which is
only two miles from Petra. Now, in the present day, airplanes carry tourists and set them down right in the middle of Petra. Every
once in a while you read an article about this amazing place. People wonder about it, but it is soon forgotten.

In the Scripture quoted above, it mentions that God is
going to take the remnant of Jews left in Palestine at the time of
the great battle of Armageddon, and the beginning of the terrible
Tribulation, to a place He has prepared for them and keep them
safely until all this trouble is over. It also says He is going
to take them on the wings of two eagles. Two of God's own spaceships? Two great jets? These two vehicles will have to be big
enough to carry 144,000 people, because the Bible tells us that is
how many are going to be saved from this awful holocaust.

W. E. Blackstone, who wrote JESUS IS COMING!, which is
one of the greatest books about the Second Coming of Jesus, was so
certain that Petra was the place God had prepared for these Jewish
people that he had 144,000 New Testaments vacuum sealed in cans and
shipped to Petra. They are stored there in one of the many buildings carved out of solid rock. He wanted these Jews to have the
New Testament that tells of Jesus being the Messiah during the three
and one-half years they will be kept there -- for the period mentioned in the quoted portion from Revelation is three and one-half
years.

The entrance to Petra is Es Siq, which means "a cleft,"
and that is all it is. It is very narrow, being only twenty feet
wide at its narrowest point, and is 6,000 feet long. It is a cleft
in the mountain, and the sides are so high that men appear as mere
ants going along the narrow, winding trail. As Petra proper is approached the trail narrows to where only one person at a time can
get through. One man could successfully defend Petra from attack.
It is an impregnable stronghold so far as ground attack goes.

When the glories of this beautiful Rock City (for this is
one of the names for this unique place) bursts upon one's eyesight,
it is almost unbelievable. The marble is striated in every hue,
ranging from cream to a deep red. The opening, the middle of which
is traversed by a stream, and bounded on each side by an avenue,
has a mountain range completely surrounding it. The buildings are
carved in this range, and open onto the area.

The city has a very unusual water supply which originated
under the mountain on the eastern side, and after it had supplied
Petra through a system of basins, water runlets, aqueducts, reser-
voirs and cisterns, fell over the side of the cliff onto the desert -- but the hot sun had it evaporated before it hit the desert
floor. So the water supply was for, and will be for, Petra only.

Time and space will not permit my describing the glorious buildings. NATIONAL GEOGRAPHIC Magazine, in the February, 1935, issue, gives a marvelous description, and presents many colored illustrations of this place.

I do want to say something about the Eagle that has been carved in the side of the rock cliff. It is huge, and done in intricate detail. It is poised exactly like our American eagle on our great seal of the United States, which is repeated on our one-dollar bills. Strange, indeed! What machinery, or instruments were used to do all this carving? And WHO DID IT?

It is described as the Rose Rock City, half as old as time! Did people from another planet carve out all these buildings, and the huge amphitheatre, out of solid marble? Well, we just don't know, but we are loath to think that some prehistoric people could have done something we cannot do today. I would much rather ascribe it to visitors from other planets.

Speaking of the Great Seal of the United States, there is a mystery connected with it. Let's look at it a moment. It has an eagle on the obverse (front) side, and an Egyptian pyramid on the other, or reverse, side. On the obverse side, the circle above the head of the eagle has thirteen "pieces argent"; the breast has a shield with thirteen stripes; the right talon holds an olive branch with thirteen leaves; the left talon holds thirteen arrows. The Latin words, "E Pluribus Unum," is on the ribbon around the neck, and is translated, "out of many one," or "One out of many," meaning, of course, one union out of many states. On the reverse side is an unfinished Egyptian pyramid. The capstone is above it, not yet put in place, and the "glory," or burst of light surrounding it, contains an eye, symbolic of the all-seeing eye of God; and the words, "Annuit Coptis," above it, which translated mean, "He (God) has prospered our beginnings." The numerals at the base are "1776." Below this are the words, "Novis Ordo Seclorum," meaning, "A New Order of the Ages," or "A mighty order of the ages lives anew," or "An ancient order is born again."

All of this is odd. How did an Egyptian pyramid get on our most significant symbol? This Great Seal is applied to about 3,000 documents annually, including presidential proclamations, ratifications of treaties, commissions of cabinet members and ambassadors, etc., on which documents only the obverse side of the Seal is applied. However, BOTH sides appear on our one-dollar bill, probably the most common piece of exchange we have.

Do you know who designed this Great Seal? Of course you don't. Neither does anyone else. The Continental Congress had asked Benjamin Franklin, Thomas Jefferson, and John Adams to arrange for a seal for the United States of America (then consisting of only thirteen states). Well, the three men met and conferred, and pondered. None of the designs they created, or which were submitted to them were suitable. The time was drawing close when they must submit their final design.

Fairly late at night, after working on the project all day, Jefferson walked out into the cool night air of the garden to clear his mind. In a few minutes he rushed back into the room, crying jubilantly, "I have it! I have it!" Indeed, he did have some plans in his hands. They were the plans showing the Great Seal as we know it today.

Asked how he got the plans, Jefferson told a strange story. A man approached him wearing a black cloak that practically covered him, face and all, and told him that he (the strange visitor) knew they were trying to devise a Seal, and that he had a design which was appropriate and meaningful. Jefferson liked the plans immediately, and was in such a hurry to show them to the other two that he rushed back into the house without even saying, "Thank you," to the stranger.

After the excitement died down, the three went out into the garden to find the stranger, but he was gone.

Thus, NEITHER THESE FOUNDING FATHERS, NOR ANYBODY ELSE, EVER KNEW JUST WHO REALLY DESIGNED THE GREAT SEAL OF THE UNITED STATES!

THE BOOK OF JOSHUA

CHAPTER 1

NOW after the death of Moses the servant of the LORD it came to pass, that the LORD spake unto Joshua the son of Nun, Moses' minister, saying,

2 Moses my servant is dead; now therefore arise, go over this Jordan, thou, and all this people, unto the land which I do give to them, *even* to the children of Israel.

3 Every place that the sole

days ye shall pass over this Jordan, to go in to possess the land, which the LORD your God giveth you to possess it.

12 ¶ And to the Reubenites, and to the Gadites, and to half the tribe of Mă-năs'-sĕh, spake Joshua, saying,

13 Remember the word which Moses the servant of the LORD commanded you, saying, The LORD your God hath given you rest.

WHEN THE SUN STOOD STILL

Joshua was the one chosen to lead the Israelites into Canaan. Moses had disobeyed God, and while he was allowed to look over into this enchanted land (or at least it was "enchanted" to the Hebrew), he was not allowed to actually go into it. Joshua was certainly a good man, and a worthy leader. He is the only man in history who was able to control the sun and moon.

The Israelites had made an agreement with the Gibeonites, against the express wish of God, and now of course the Gibeonites were trying to overcome the Israelites and prevent them from going into Canaan. But God was definitely on the side of the Israelites, and sent His spaceships which -- but read (Joshua 10:10-14): "And the Lord discomfited them before Israel, and slew them with a great slaughter at Gibeon, and chased them along the way that goeth up to Beth-horon, and smote them to Azekah, and unto Makkedah. And it came to pass, as they fled from before Israel, and were in the

Angels surround the Christ figure in this Orthodox painting
as he descends from the sky in a circular globe.
What made this artist from the 16th Century render such a scene?

going down to Beth-horon, that the Lord <u>cast</u> <u>down</u> <u>great</u> <u>stones</u> <u>from</u> <u>heaven</u> <u>upon</u> <u>them</u> unto Azekah, and they died; they were more which died with hailstones than they whom the children of Israel slew with the sword. Then spake Joshua to the Lord in the day when the Lord delivered up the Amorites before the children of Israel, and he said in the sight of Israel, 'Sun stand thou still upon Gibeon: and thou, Moon, in the valley of Ajalon.! And the sun stood still, and the moon stayed, until the people had avenged themselves unto their enemies. Is this not written in the book of Jasher? So the sun stood still in the midst of heaven, and hasted not to go down about a whole day. And there was no day like that before it or after it, that the Lord hearkened unto the voice of one man: for the Lord fought for Israel."

Of course, we all know that it is the earth that turns, or rotates, on its axis. So we say that the Bible is in error when it says that Joshua commanded the "Sun, stand thou still...."
However, the word in the original is "Sun, cease working." It is the magnetic action of the sun that causes the earth to rotate, so if the sun "ceased working," the earth would quit rotating.

Immanuel Velikovsky in his book, WORLDS IN COLLISION, tells, on pages 44-45, of the research he did in the Western Hemisphere in regard to this prolonged day. He reasoned that if there was a prolonged day in the Eastern Hemisphere, there would certainly be a correspondingly prolonged night in the Western Hemisphere. He found that this was so.

What kind of "anti-rotational" means was used to stop the earth in its rotation? Some powerful magnetic means was applied to bring about this miracle. I know it happened -- the Bible says so. And other historical records say so also.

I not only like to contemplate the FACT of this stupendous occurrence, I love the poetry of it: ".....and thou, Moon, in the valley of Ajalon." Just say those words out loud and hear how beautiful they are.

Also, you will remember, it was Joshua who made the recording of the Israelites making a covenant to obey God, and then told them that this recording would be a witness against them if they failed. The recording was made on the ever-present Bethel Stone, as told about earlier in this manuscript.

Sometimes I wonder if God doesn't have some type of tape recording of each of us which will be used at the Judgment either to "accuse or excuse" us. It is perfectly possible. We stand in Church and take vows -- maybe the stones in the building are recording them. Whew!

The account in Joshua goes thus (Joshua 24:22-27): "And Joshua said unto the people, 'Ye are witnesses against yourselves that ye have chosen you the Lord, to serve him.' And they said, 'We are witnesses.' 'Now therefore put away,' said he, 'the strange gods which are among you, and incline your heart unto the Lord God of

Israel.' And the people said unto Joshua, 'The Lord our God will we serve, and his voice will we obey.' So Joshua made a covenant with the people that day, and set them a statute and an ordinance in Shechem. And Joshua wrote these words in the book of the law of God, and took the great stone, and set it up under an oak, that was by the sanctuary of the Lord. And Joshua said unto all the people, 'Behold, this stone shall be a witness unto us; for it has heard all the words of the Lord which he spake unto us: it shall be therefore a witness unto you, lest ye deny your God.'"

THE SECOND BOOK OF SAMUEL

CHAPTER 1

NOW it came to pass after the ...vid was ...of the ...bode

...third ...e out ...h his ...h his ...came ...arth,

7 And when he looked behind him, he saw me, and called unto me. And I answered, Here *am* I.

8 And he said unto me, Who *art* thou? And I answered him, I *am* an Ä-mǎl'-ĕk-ite.

9 He said unto me again, Stand, I pray thee, upon me, and slay me: for anguish is come upon me, because my life *is* yet whole in me.

10 So I stood upon him, and slew him, because I was sure that h... could not li...

THE FIRST BOOK OF SAMUEL

CHAPTER 1

NOW there was a certain man of Rā-mǎ-thā'-im-zophim, of mount Ē'-phrǎ-im, and his name *was* Ĕl-kā'-nǎh, the son of Jĕ-rō'-hǎm, the son of Ē-lī'-hū, the son of Tohu... of Zuph, an ĕph'-rǎ-...

indeed look on the affliction of thine handmaid, and remember me, and not forget thine handmaid, but wilt give unto thine handmaid a man child, then I will give him unto the LORD all the days of his life, and there shall no razor come upon his head.

...it came to pass as she...

THE SOUND OF A GOING

In First Samuel we have an account of the Ark of the Covenant being taken from its rightful place and of the dire happenings accompanying the handling of it. The Ark of the Covenant, or Testimony, was the central object of the Tabernacle in the wilderness. It was made of acacia wood covered with pure gold within and without. A rim or molding of gold encircled it at the top. At the bottom were two golden rings on each side, through which poles of acacia wood overlaid with gold were put for the purpose of carrying the Ark about. It was covered with a lid of solid gold which was called the Mercy Seat. Two cherubim of gold stood on the cover, and were made of one piece with it, one at each end facing each other and looking down at the Mercy Seat. Wonder where they got so much gold? It stood in the Holy of Holies of the Tabernacle, in which no natural light entered, and it was from between the Cherubim that the voice of God came in answer to the high priest when he used the Urim and Thummim for a consultation. Somehow this was a kind of receiving set, or two-way radio. After the priesthood became so decadent, and was no longer powerful in Israel, the Urim and Thummim disappeared from sight, and we no longer hear of these strange consultations.

The Ark of the Covenant was made especially as a receptacle for the two tables of stone on which the Ten Commandments were inscribed. It also contained Aaron's rod that budded, and was miraculous indeed; and a pot of manna that fell from heaven to feed the Israelites during the time on the desert when they had nothing to eat, but which spoiled when not consumed in one day. However, this pot of manna presumably stayed fresh and sweet in the Ark of the Covenant for as long as it stayed there -- what kept it fresh?

In First Samuel we also have the account of the Ark's falling into the hands of the enemy. They soon found out they had a "hot potato." For when not carried properly (by the poles) it was very dangerous. Anyone who touched the Ark per se would die (radiation poisoning?). The Ark was placed in the Holy of Holies of Solomon's temple, but disappeared when Jerusalem was destroyed by Nebuchadnezzar, and has not been heard of since.

Of interest to the students of the occult is the account in the 28th Chapter of Second Samuel of how Saul prevailed upon the witch of Endor to call up Samuel for him. I do not know what to think of this chapter. Again, I know it happened -- the Bible says so. However, I do not think God intends for us to dabble in these things, as he very definitely punished Saul for doing this thing. Also, the Bible tells us that it was only after Saul had lost his contact with God, and had disobeyed Him so much that he could get no audience with God, that he hunted out the "familiar spirit" to try to get help. In First Chronicles 10:13-14, we are told, "So Saul died for his transgression which he committed against the Lord, even against the word of the Lord, which he kept not, and also for asking counsel of one that had a familiar spirit, to inquire of it; and inquired not of the Lord: therefore he slew him, and turned the kingdom unto David the son of Jesse."

David had an experience which must have involved a "flying saucer." The story is told in II Samuel. David was at war with the seemingly ever-present Philistines, and was approaching a particular strategic battle. The Ark of the Covenant was at one of the Israelites' homes, there being no temple or tabernacle at this time.

David had access to it, and as the Bible relates it, he could also get a response to his questions. Well, anyway, his instructions for this particular battle were as follows:

"And when David inquired of the Lord, he said Thou shalt not go up; but fetch a compass behind them, and come upon them over against the mulberry trees. And let it be, when thou hearest the sound of a going in the tops of the mulberry trees, that then thou shalt bestir thyself: for then shall the Lord go out before thee, to smite the host of the Philistines. And David did so, as the Lord had commanded him; and smote the Philistines from Geba until thou come to Gazer." (II Samuel 5: 23-24)

From their vantage point in the sky, the visitors could see just what the Philistines were doing, and when the moment came that was propitious for the Israelites to strike, they just hovered over the grove of mulberry trees and made them quiver, as it had been pre-arranged with David.

ROUND TRIP BY SAUCER

nother incident connected with the Ark of the Covenant is related in First Kings. When Solomon built the temple--- and what a wondrous building it was -- and the grand day came when it was completed, and the mysterious Ark of the

Covenant was placed in it as an act of dedication during the first public service that was held, "And the priests brought in the ark of the covenant of the Lord unto his place, into the oracle of the house, to the most holy place, even under the wings of the cherubim.....there was nothing in the Ark save the two tables of stone, which Moses put there at Horeb, when the Lord made a covenant with the children of Israel, when they came out of the land of Egypt. And it came to pass, when the priests were come out of the holy place, that the cloud filled the house of the Lord, so that the priests could not stand to minister because of the cloud: for the glory of the Lord had filled the house of the Lord."

How about that? The force from this comparatively small UFO which had entered into the main court of the temple was so powerful that the priests could not stand up to minister. The sacrifice was offered in the courtyard of the temple, which was part of the temple. By "comparatively small," I mean small in comparison with the tremendously large spaceship that traveled with the Israelites through the desert.

We have another description of the dedication of the temple and the cloud in II Chronicles, Chapter 5. And in the seventh chapter we are told that following Solomon's sermon of the sixth chapter, that, "Now when Solomon had made an end of praying, the fire came down from heaven, and consumed the burnt offering and the sacrifices; and the glory of the Lord filled the house. And the priests could not enter into the house of the Lord, because the glory of the Lord had filled the Lord's house. And when all the children of Israel saw how the fire came down, and the glory of the Lord upon the house, they bowed themselves with their faces to the ground upon the pavement, and worshipped, and praised the Lord, saying, For he is good; for his mercy endureth for ever."

Then, that night, Solomon had an extra-terrestrial visitor, who ratified to him a covenant made with David, his father. Among other things, he said, "If my people, which are called by my name, shall humble themselves, and pray, and seek my face, and turn from their wicked ways; then will I hear from heaven, and will forgive their sin, and will heal their land." This message from God to Solomon is very timely for us today.

Solomon was the richest man that ever lived, I suppose, and certainly he was the wisest. The Bible says so. "So King Solomon exceeded all the kings of the earth for riches and for wisdom." He even knew the secret of nuclear fission (recorded in the uncanonized books of the Bible), but it evidently died with him. Einstein was a very wise man himself. He was the one that brought this knowledge back to man, but I am afraid it was a knowledge we could have well done without.

But for all his wisdom, Solomon was not smart enough to cope with women, and they became his downfall. "But Solomon loved many strange women." He had been warned that they would turn his heart away from the true God to idolatry, for each of these "strange" women had her own particular god, and in order to completely pos-

ELIJAH WAS TRANSPORTED TO THE KINGDOM OF GOD IN A CHARIOT OF FIRE

sess Solomon, it was natural that she would insist on his accepting her god along with her. It happened that way: "....and his wives turned away his heart."

Imagine, following an experience like the one at the dedication of the temple, to turn away from a power like that to idolatry, just to please a woman!

Second Kings contains the story of Elijah. The most outstanding thing about Elijah was the way he left this earth, for after a varied and colorful, to say the least, life, he was taken away in a "chariot of fire....by a whirlwind." This we are told in II Kings 2:11.

Elijah seemed to know he was going to have this spectacular ending, because he had promised his close companion, Elisha, that if he should be present and see him when he was taken away, that a "double portion" of his spirit would fall upon the latter, and that Elisha would be able to preach like he did and do the miraculous things that he had done. Well, Elisha certainly intended to have his heritage and would not let Elijah out of his sight for a minute, until one day he saw this wonderful, glowing, flashing, fiery vehicle (what other word did he have but "chariot" for a means of transportation?) and cried, "....My father, my father, the chariot of Israel."
Could it have been the same "pillar of cloud" that had guided and protected the Children of Israel during their desert wanderings? Is it not reasonable to suppose that this marvelous story had been handed down from father to son, and had been described over and over, until the minute Elisha saw it, he recognized it?

At any rate, no matter what you call it, it WAS A SPACESHIP. It took Elijah from earth to heaven.

Elijah had probably seen this craft before, and communed with its Pilot. He certainly was very sure that some day he would depart this life in it, because he had warned Elisha about being watchful in order to see him when he went.

Elijah was familiar with heavenly "fire." Remember the altar he built and poured water around it, and after he prayed, fire came down from heaven and consumed his offering and licked up the water. Another time (II Kings 1:10 and 12) he asked for fire from heaven to consume a captain and his band of fifty soldiers, and his request was granted -- twice. Where did it come from? Elijah was in pretty close communion with the "Sender" of this fire, and so he knew that some day this craft was going to pick him up and take him to heaven without his experiencing death.

Well, it did. Not only that, Elijah made a round trip. He was present on the Mount of Transfiguration with Jesus and Moses, and was recognized by Peter, James and John (Matthew 17:3).

Now let us think for a moment about the servant of Elisha.

He really had an envied experience. Syria was warring against the Israelites, and during the night had surrounded the city in great force. The servant quaked, and asked his master what they should do. Elisha answered with a truism that should impress itself upon our minds and hearts today: "Fear not: for they that be with us are more than they that be with them." (II Kings 6:15-17). For even one plus God is a majority.

So Elijah prayed that God might open the eyes of the young man, and the servant saw that "the mountains was full of horses and chariots of fire round about Elisha." Think of how amazed that young man must have been upon seeing a host of craft covering the heavens! From this account it would seem that our relationship with God determines, to a measure anyway, just how much of God's glory we are able to apprehend or "see." The servant could only see the fiery vehicles after Elisha had prayed and asked God to "open his eyes." They were evidently very plain to Elisha all the time. He certainly knew they were there.

In modern times we read of the "flying saucers" being able to materialize and dematerialize.

THE BOOK OF JOB

CHAPTER 1

THERE was a man in the land of Uz, whose name *was* Job; and that man was perfect and upright, and one that feared God, and es-

2 And there were born unto him seven sons and three daughters.
3 His substance also was seven thousand sheep, and three thousand camels, and five hundred yoke of oxen, and five hundred she asses,

OUT OF THE WHIRLWIND

Poor Job! He was probably the most harrassed man of record in the Bible, and yet, when you come to think of it, he was selected for the most signal honor of any man in history. Job was a good man. Every morning he got up early and prayed for every one of his children, calling them by name before God. Even if he did not know of anything wicked they had done, he prayed for them anyway, just in case they really had done something.

In this oldest written manuscript of which we have any record, we read some marvelous things. Even in the first chapter we have an account of a conference, or meeting of the universal chiefs, INCLUDING Satan. There he was, right among them.

God asked him, "Whence comest thou?" and Satan answered, "From going to and fro in the earth, and from walking up and down in it."

From the next question God put to him, we have the inference that Satan's business in walking up and down, to and fro in the earth, was to try to ensnare everyone he could. The question God asked him was, "Hast thou considered my servant Job, that there is none like him in the earth, a PERFECT and upright man, one that feareth God, and escheweth evil?"

Satan is cynical now, as then -- listen to his answer: "Doth Job fear God for nought? Hast not thou made an hedge about him, and about his house, and about all that he hath on every side? Thou has blessed the work of his hands, and his substance is increased in the land. But put forth thine hand now, and touch all that he hath, and he will curse thee to thy face."

Well, God accepted the challenge Satan extended because He had great faith in Job. He knew that no matter what Satan did to him, Job would remain faithful to Him. So God told Satan, "Behold, all that he hath is in thy power; only upon himself put not forth thine hand."

That was all Satan wanted -- at that time. However, he found out that Job put so little value on material things, that he went on blessing God even after they were lost. So Satan went back to the next meeting held in space (I am sure he used some kind of UFO to travel those vast distances), and asked for permission to attack Job personally. This permission was granted, but Job never yielded, and was victorious to the eternal glory of God. Down to this day he has remained an encouragement to believers. It can be done.

Job was not only good; he was wise, or at any rate, he possessed what seemed to be unlimited knowledge. We are just now finding out things that Job knew about. For instance, in the 26th chapter he said, "He (referring to God) stretcheth out the north over the empty place, and hangeth the earth upon nothing." For hundreds of years people thought the earth was supported in some manner. Job knew it wasn't. As for the empty place over the north, how about the recent theory that the point of greatest magnetic power is a RING and not just one point -- and that this ring surrounds an OPENING into the earth? It just might be so. And how about this (38th) chapter: "When I made the cloud the garment thereof, and thick darkness a swaddlingband for it, and brake up for it my de- creed place, and set bars and doors, and said, Hitherto shalt thou come, but no further."

Certainly it was only recently that Dr. Van Allen discovered the tremendous belt of radiation that surrounds the earth like a swaddlingband, or doughnut, and that the North and South Poles are free of this radiation; and he voiced the opinion that if ever we sent men into space, it would have to be via one of these routes to avoid the radiation. Job knew about the swaddlingband or belt of radiation; he also knew that it would serve as a "bar" to too much space investigation before God was ready for us to do this; and he also knew that there was an opening or "door" through which it would be safe for one to go and not encounter the deadly radia- tion.

Incidentally, in the first verse of the 38th chapter, we have this statement: "Then the Lord answered Job out of the <u>whirlwind</u> and said....." The word "whirlwind" is the word from which we get "dynamite" or "power." It was a conveyance powered by something we just don't know anything about that brought the outer-space visitor to Job. This is also the word used for the spaceship that took Elijah to heaven.

I am loath to leave Job without describing the keen insight he had in spiritual matters, but this book is about "flying saucers" and other strange related subjects, so I will hasten on.

THE BOOK OF PSALMS

PSALM 1

BLESSED *is* the man that walketh not in the counsel of the ungodly, nor standeth in the way of sinners, nor sitteth in the seat of the scornful.

2 But his delight *is* in the law of the LORD; and in his law doth he

8 Ask of me, and I shall give *thee* the heathen *for* thine inheritance, and the uttermost parts of the earth *for* thy possession.

9 Thou shalt break them with a rod of iron; thou shalt dash them in pieces like a potter's vessel.

10 Be wise now therefore, O ye kings: be in

THE WORLD'S FIRST AIRLIFT

Although the Bible is not a textbook on science, it is scientifically correct; and while it is not a textbook on history, it is historically correct; and we could go on and on, naming the many ways in which the Bible is meticulously correct. The Psalms are usually used as devotional material, and so they are; but there are many startling passages in this book, which, if analyzed and thought about, give us scientific and historical facts that amaze us.

In the historical passage known as Psalm 78, beginning with the 19th verse, there is a question that sums up the complaining and murmurings of the Israelites while enroute over the desert (on which they spent forty years because of their perverseness, when forty <u>days</u> of consistent, orderly travel probably would have brought them into Canaan). The question is: "Can God furnish a table in the wilderness?" In other words, can He feed us out there in that barren place? Well, He not only could, He DID.

How? God summoned his space ships and loaded them with supplies from His particular abode and took it over the desert where the Israelites were and dropped it down to them: the first airlift of which we have any record!

Before we quote the passages dealing with the airlift, notice first that He provided water (Verse 20): "Behold, he smote <u>the rock</u>, that waters gushed out, and the streams overflowed; can he give bread also? can he provide flesh for his people?" Note the definite article, "the," before "rock" -- not just a rock, but the rock. Now read Verses 23-29: "Though he had commanded the clouds from above, and opened the doors of heaven, and had rained down manna upon them to eat, and had given them of the corn of heaven, Man did eat angels' food: he sent them meat to the full......He rained flesh also upon them as dust, and feathered fowls like as the sand of the sea: (remember the quail???) and he let it fall in the midst of their camp, round about their habitations. So they did eat, and were well filled: for he gave them their own desire."

Isn't that amazing? You may object that the "clouds" mentioned are just that -- but did you ever see ordinary clouds rain manna? Of course not. I repeat, that the only word they had for large, grey objects, going, or standing still, in the atmosphere, was clouds.

And how about the phrase, "Man did eat angels' food."? This is a record of food that is eaten on other planets, and even maybe in other galaxies, being brought to earth for consumption of earth people. It must have been very nutritious, too, for it was all they had at that time, and they thrived on it.

Then the majestic 104th Psalm: "Bless the Lord, O my soul, O Lord my God, thou art very great; thou art clothed with honour and majesty. Who coverest thyself with LIGHT as with a garment; who stretchest out the heavens like a curtain: who layeth the beams of his chambers in the waters (firmament): WHO MAKETH THE CLOUDS HIS CHARIOTS: Who walketh upon the wings of the wind: who maketh his angels spirits; his ministers a flaming fire; who laid the foundations of the earth, that it should not be removed forever. Thou coveredst it with the deep as with a garment; the waters stood above the mountains.....Thou hast set a bound that they may not pass over; that they turn not again to cover the earth."

Let's examine this passage. "Clothed with light" -- we are told that that is to be our garment in heaven. Remember that light conceals while it reveals. I can remember when our light bulbs were just clear glass, and when not burning, one could see the naked wires inside. But turn the light on, and the wires could not be seen. They were clothed with light. At any rate, we won't have a laundry problem!

"Who maketh the clouds his chariot" -- Here we have a definite statement that these so-called "clouds" are God's means of transportation for Himself and His hosts. Remember, God is a Spirit, although He is a definite Personality. Only in His Son Jesus do we actually, physically "see God." However, there are many accounts of theophanies (appearance of God in a body) in the Bible. Remember the three men who visited Abraham, and the Bible definitely says that one of them was the LORD. In the Old Testament when the word "Lord" is all in capital, or upper case, letters, it is the word for God the Son, or Christ of the New Testament. I cannot go into this, but any Bible scholar can tell you the same thing. So, when we read that the voice of God spoke out of the spaceship, it

was the voice of God the Son. However, his hosts, cherubim, sera-
phim, angels, and so on, are really embodied entities, and would
necessarily have to employ a material means of transportation.

In this passage we also have the statement that He set bounds
for the oceans and seas. I have seen the tide come in, rush up on
the beach -- just so far -- and then recede. Never did it go beyond the bounds. I could not understand this as a child, but after
reading this in the Bible I knew why -- God had set the bounds for
the waters.

I urge you to read this entire 104th Psalm. It will make you
think upon the wisdom, goodness, and might of God.

THE BOOK OF THE PROPHET

ISAIAH

CHAPTER 1

THE vision of Isaiah the son of Amoz, which he saw concerning Judah and Jerusalem in the days of Ŭz-zi'-ăh, Jotham, Ahaz, *and* Hĕz-ē-kī'-ăh, kings of Judah.

2 Hear, O heavens, and give ear, O earth: for the LORD hath spoken, I have nourished and brought up children, and they have rebelled

3 The ox knoweth his owner, and the ass his master's crib: *but* Israel doth not know, my people doth not consider.

4 Ah sinful nation, a people laden with iniquity, a seed of evildoers, children that are corrupters: they have forsaken the LORD, they have provoked the Holy One of Israel unto anger, they are gone away

PROPHECY FULFILLED

Isaiah was foremost among the writing prophets. There might have been greater prophets, but certainly not in the realm of writings. Isaiah was the prophet who predicted the birth of Christ in the beautiful passage of Scripture we use so often at Christmas time: "For unto us a child is born, unto us a son is given: and the government shall be upon his shoulder: and his name shall be called Wonderful, Counsellor, The mighty God, The everlasting Father, the Prince of Peace." He also promises him the throne of David, which shall never cease.

This eternal throne of David may have seemed rather empty during the hundreds of years that Israel was not even a nation. When
Jerusalem was destroyed in 70 A.D., all the records were done away
with that pertained to the succession of the throne. Both Joseph
and Mary were of the lineage of David, and of course, Jesus. When
the records were destroyed, Jesus was the last one of record quali-
fied to inherit the throne.

But May, 1948, brought a dramatic happening to the world. It
was then that Israel was declared a nation, recognized by the United
Nations, and the flag of David was hoisted over that portion of Palestine controlled by the Hebrews, after hundreds of years. It was
a most unlikely thing, but it happened. Israel was a nation!

This one thing is the key to prophecy regarding the return of the Lord. The generation that sees this thing come to pass will also be the generation to witness the return of the Lord.

Isaiah also prophesied regarding the Kingdom Age. Read Isaiah 2:2-4. This passage is word for word the same as the passage in Micah 4:1-3. Why? It was such an important matter that God inspired two of his prophets to write the same thing. "In the mouth of two or three witnesses shall every word be established." (Matthew 18:16).
Among other things, this passage tells us that Jerusalem shall be the world center for government. Palestine was not a happenstance with God. If you will take a compass and place it on Jerusalem and make a circle, you will find that Jerusalem is the dead land center of the earth. "I have placed thee in the midst of the nations." Not only will it be the political center of the earth, but also the religious center.

"Flying Saucers" in Isaiah? I'll say! Just read Isaiah 6:1-8: "In the year that king Uzziah died I saw also the Lord sitting upon a throne, high and lifted up, and his train filled the temple. Above it stood the seraphims: each one had six wings; with twain he covered his face, and with twain he covered his feet, and with twain he did fly. And one cried to another, and said, Holy, holy, holy, is the Lord of hosts: the whole earth is full of his glory. And the posts of the door moved at the voice of him that cried, and the house was filled with smoke. Then said I, Woe is me! for I am undone; because I am a man of unclean lips, and I dwell in the midst of a people of unclean lips: for mine eyes have seen the King, the Lord of hosts. Then flew one of the seraphims unto me, having a live coal in his hand, which he had taken with the tongs from off the altar: and he laid it upon my mouth, and said, Lo, this hath touched thy lips; and thine iniquity is taken away, and thy sin purged. Also I heard the voice of the Lord, saying, Whom shall I send, and who will go for us? Then said I, Here am I; send me."

This is an account of quite a few UFO coming at the same time. Evidently one of them landed, because one of the visitors came right up to Isaiah. Then the voice asking for a volunteer to give the message to the people. I have to laugh when I think of the reception the people gave Isaiah's message when he told them how he got it. "I was contacted by space people," he would have to say. I guess they all thought he was crazy. That's what happens to a "contactee" in this day and time. However, the times are so desperate that I guess God will have to use desperate measures again to get our attention. Hence the UFO.

In Isaiah 60:8, he asked this question: "Who are these that fly as a cloud?" We ask the same question: "What planet are they from? Who are they?"

In the 19th chapter we have what is generally believed to be a reference to the great Pyramid of Gizeh in Egypt. Many scholars think Melchisedek was the architect for this pyramid, and that Melchisedek was one of the manifestations of Christ. Therefore, Christ was the Architect of the Pyramid of Gizeh. The scripture goes like this: "In that day shall there be an altar to the Lord in the midst of the land of Egypt, and a pillar at the border thereof to the Lord. And it shall be for a sign and for a witness unto the Lord of hosts in the land of Egypt....And the Lord shall be known in Egypt, and the Egyptian shall know the Lord in that day ....In that day shall there be a highway out of Egypt to Assyria, and the Assyrian shall come into Egypt, and the Egyptian into Assyria, and the Egyptians shall serve with the Assyrians. In that day shall Israel be the third with Egypt and with Assyria, even a blessing in the midst of the land."

This highway was completed in July, 1933. It makes access between Egypt and Assyria easy. I read an editorial in the morning paper about Nasser of Egypt and his Arab allies. I suppose that is why I included this passage.

THE BOOK OF THE PROPHET EZEKIEL

CHAPTER 1

NOW it came to pass in the thirtieth year, in the fourth *month*, in the fifth *day* of the month, as I *was* among the captives by the river of Che'-bär, *that* the heavens were opened, and I saw visions of God.

2 In the fifth *day* of the month,

and the hand of the LORD was there upon him.

4 ¶ And I looked, and, behold, a whirlwind came out of the north, a great cloud, and a fire infolding itself, and a brightness *was* about it, and out of the midst thereof as the colour of amber, out of the midst of the fire.

5 Also out of the midst thereof

A CLASSIC SAUCER

The Book of Ezekiel is a classic as far as flying saucers are concerned. Beginning with the very first chapter, which gives a detailed description of a "flying saucer," it continues with a very human story of how this means of transportation was provided for Ezekiel to go to Jerusalem and deliver a message to the remnant that was left there after the most of the Israelites had been carried captive by Nebuchadnezzar to Babylon. The huge flying ship hovered over Jerusalem and waited until he had delivered his message and then it took him back to Babylon. This message, or a series of messages, are recorded, and constitute the greater part of the book.

Nebuchadnezzar besieged the city of Jerusalem three times, and took captives each time. It was during the second siege that Ezekiel was taken to Babylon. This particular foray of Nebuchadnezzar is told in II Kings 24:11-16: "And Nebuchadnezzar king of Babylon came against the city, and his servants did besiege it. And Jehoichin the king of Judah went out to the king of Babylon, he, and his mother, and his servants, and his princes, and his officers: and the king of Babylon took him in the eighth year of his reign. And he carried out thence all the treasures of the house of the Lord, and the treasures of the king's house, and cut in pieces all the vessels of gold which Solomon king of Israel had made in the temple of the Lord, as the Lord had said. And he carried away all Jerusalem, and all the princes, and all the mighty men of valour, even ten thousand captives, all the craftsmen and smiths: none remained, save the poorest sort of the people of the land....."

Well, the Israelites (or rather Judah, the southern kingdom) began to marry and make homes in Babylon. Too, they liked the big city, and all its conveniences, pomp, and display, and pretty soon they forgot their pastoral way of living in Palestine; they forgot about the seventh day belonging to God (so do we), and they forgot to tithe (so do we), and they "forsook the assembling of themselves together" in the temple (so do we), and all in all, they became a pretty sorry lot. Smarter, maybe, in the ways of the world.

There were a few exceptions, however, such as Daniel and the three princes. Daniel was such an exceptional person that he became advisor to the king. Ezekiel was one of these. He was a godly man, and it grieved his heart that the Israelites were growing more and more cold toward their high calling of showing the world that there was one true God.

Not only was Ezekiel grieved about the sad state of affairs in Babylon, he worried even more about the remnant that had been left in Palestine. As the Bible tells us, they were the poorest of the land -- poorest in ambition, I guess -- and as they had been left in Palestine without a leader, and under the influence of the occupational army left by Nebuchadnezzar, Ezekiel was rightly worried. This remnant fraternized with the soldiers left over them, and intermarried. The descendants of these marriages became the hated Samaritans of the New Testament, and the Jews would not even go through their territory when going from North to South, or vice versa, in Palestine, but would cross the Jordan and go up its eastern side which was a very round-about way, rather than contact the Samaritans.

Well, one day when Ezekiel had been in Babylon a little more than thirty years, he was sitting by the river Chebar and he looked up and there was a "flying saucer."

"And I looked, and behold, a whirlwind (powerful, dynamic) came out of the north, a great cloud, and a fire infolding itself, and a brightness was about it, and out of the midst thereof as the color of amber, out of the midst of the fire. Also, out of the midst thereof came the likeness of four living creatures. This was their appearance; they had the likeness of a man...... And their feet were straight feet; and the sole of their feet was like the sole of a calf's foot: and they sparkled like the colour of burnished brass. And they had the hands of a man under their wings on their four sides; and they four had their faces and their wings. Their wings were joined one to another (like mountain climbers, for protection?); they turned not when they went; they went every one straight forward......As for the likeness of the living creatures, their appearance was like burning coals of fire, and like the appearance of lamps: it (the UFO) went up and down among the living creatures; (like a ball bouncing, I would think, as it hovered) and the fire was bright, and out of the fire went forth lightning (It certainly was bright). Now as I beheld the living creatures, behold one wheel upon the earth, by the living creatures. The ap-

pearance of the wheels and their work was like unto the color of a
beryl: and they four had one likeness (they all had on the same
kind of glistening metal suits): and their appearance and their
work was as it were a wheel in the middle of a wheel. (The UFO
had a rim on the outer periphery which rotated.) When they went,
they went upon their four sides: and they turned not when they
went (Ezekiel is describing what we have often heard about the UFO.
They turn at right angles -- go in a straight line. Also, he refers
to the UFO with a plural word -- no wonder -- he thought it was
plural, I guess, with a "wheel within a wheel" and the next verse,
which says it had "eyes" or portholes). As for their rings, they
were so high that they were dreadful; and their rings were full of
eyes round about them four (four portholes). And when the living
creatures went, the wheels went by them; and when the living creatures were lifted up from the earth, the wheels were lifted up.
Whithersoever the spirit (little "s" -- it was the living creatures'
spirit or will -- not God's Spirit) was to go, they went thither was
their spirit to go; and the wheels were lifted up over against them:
for the spirit of the living creatures was in the wheels (in other
words the men controlled the machine). When those went, these went;
and when those stood, these stood: and when those were lifted up
from the earth, the wheels were lifted up over against them (their landing gear was drawn up against the machine when they were airborne):
for the spirit of the living creatures was in the wheels. And the
likeness of the firmament upon the heads of the living creatures
was as the colour of the terrible crystal, stretched forth over
their heads above (They had on "crystal" or transparent helmets).
......And when they went, I heard the noise of their wings, like
the noise of great waters, as the voice of the Almighty, the voice
of speech, as the noise of an host: when they stood, they let
down their wings. And there was a voice from the firmament ("firmament" is another word for atmosphere or water. Evidently, the material from which the helmets were made was like our plastic, as it
seemed to ripple, or reflect the light. Nevertheless, it was transparent like crystal. The "voice" came from within the helmets --
that's natural, as their mouths were in their heads) that was over
their heads, when they stood, and had let down their wings (In other words, one of them spoke, after they had landed and let down some
kind of landing ramp on which they descended from the UFO)."

This spokesman out-glittered the others. He had a radiation
about him that looked like a rainbow, which must have had something
to do with the speaking apparatus. Read on: "And above the firmament that was over their heads was the likeness of a throne, as
the appearance of a sapphire stone: and upon the likeness of the
throne was the likeness as the appearance of a man above upon it.
And I saw the color of amber, as the appearance of fire round about
within it, from the appearance of his loins even downward, I saw
as it were the appearance of fire, and it had brightness round
about (His two-piece suit glowed like a neon sign. Note, also, the
mention of the "color of amber" -- this color is often mentioned in
connection with flying saucers)." "As the appearance of the bow that
is in the cloud in the day of rain, so was the appearance of the
brightness round about. This was the appearance of the likeness of
the glory of the Lord." (He did not say it was the Lord, although

it could have been. He said it was the appearance of the "glory of
the Lord." So is all nature. So is man himself -- in fact, man is
God's crowning glory of creation, but we have degraded ourselves until we are not so glorious. But certainly, this wonderful space
ship that Ezekiel is describing so perfectly and so minutely, is a
glory to the Lord.)

"And when I saw it, I fell down upon my face, and I heard a
voice of one that spake. And he said unto me, 'Son of man, stand
upon thy feet, and I will speak unto thee.'....And he said unto me,
'Son of man, I send thee to the children of Israel, to a rebellious
nation that hath rebelled against me: they and their fathers have
transgressed against me, even unto this day.'"

This visitor, the speaker for the group, made quite a speech to
Ezekiel, encouraging him to go back to Jerusalem and deliver a message that he would give him. He told Ezekiel to "eat the roll,"
or in other words, to thoroughly digest it before he went.

Ezekiel was scared half to death, but in the third chapter we
have a record of how he let the visitors entice him into the machine
and they took him for a trial run. Ezekiel says, "Then the spirit
took me up, and I heard behind me a voice of a great rushing....I
heard also the noise of the wings of the living creatures that
touched one another, and the noise of the wheels over against them,
and the noise of a great rushing. So the spirit lifted me up, and
took me away, and I went in bitterness, in the heat of my spirit;
but the hand of the Lord was strong upon me." Ezekiel was mad at
himself because he had let them over-persuade him to get in the
spaceship. But above it all, he still felt that it was his duty to
do as he was bidden.

Would you have gotten into that "thing" if it had appeared to
you there in the plains a little way from Babylon? I suspect that
I would have had to have a lot of assistance from the rear!

Just read this very ordinary and human incident that happened
next: "Then I came to them of the captivity at Tel-abib, and
dwelt by the river of Chebar, and I sat where they sat, and remained
there astonished among them seven days." Isn't this priceless? He
returned to his own little community of Tel-abib, and stayed there
for a week, never getting over his "astonishment" at what had happened so far. Do you suppose the people believed that he had really
been contacted by visitors from outer-space, and that he had taken
a ride in a flying saucer?

Well, one day, he felt impressed to go back out on the plain
where he had experienced the strange event. I am reminded of
Adamski when he felt impressed to go to the hotel where he met the
two men who took him for a ride in a flying saucer -- so he says.
I don't know whether Adamski went or not, but I am POSITIVE that
Ezekiel did. The Bible says so.

Well, as I say, he felt this compulsion to visit again the
scene of his heavenly visitation: "And the hand of the Lord was

there upon me (Tel-abib): and he said unto me, 'Arise, go forth into the plain, and I will there talk with thee'! Then I arose and went forth into the plain, and behold! the glory of the Lord stood there, as the glory which I saw by the river of Chebar: and I fell on my face." He says, that when he went to the plain, WHAT DO YOU KNOW! THERE STOOD THE UFO AGAIN. THE VERY SAME ONE HE HAD SEEN BY THE RIVER CHEBAR!

Well, a little later, he again felt compelled to go to the plain where he had seen the UFO the second time. When he reached there, they had already landed, and here was the same speaker in the glowing two-piece suit. "Then I beheld, and lo a likeness as the appearance of fire: from the appearance of his loins even downward, fire: and from his loins even upward, as the appearance of brightness, as the colour of amber."

Ezekiel had had enough of this, and as he turned to run, and his long hair flowed out in the wind, read what happened: "And he (the speaker) put forth the form of an hand, and took me by a lock of mine head: and the spirit lifted me up between the earth and the heaven, and brought me.....to Jerusalem, to the door of the inner gate that looketh toward the north; where was the seat of the image of jealousy (An idol had been set up just inside the walls of the city by the north gate)." It was here that the flying saucer let Ezekiel out.

The space ship hovered over Jerusalem and waited for Ezekiel to go to the temple area and just see what had happened to it, and the devastation in general that had been wrought in the city. I don't know whether it went back to its home base, or whether it just stayed there, but that is not important. What is important is that Ezekiel evidently stayed there for quite a few days, because the account of the messages he brought to the neglected remnant of Israel takes up the remainder of the Book of Ezekiel.

These are amazing messages, and if read carefully, one will find that not only did Ezekiel prophesy what was going to happen to Israel, but that his prophecies were much more far-reaching, and that they cover incidents and wars YET TO OCCUR.

When Ezekiel had delivered himself of his burden that was on his heart, and had preached to the people and warned them of the disaster to come if they did not change their ways, then the spaceship returned, picked Ezekiel up and took him back to Babylon. The captive Israelites needed Ezekiel's message, too, as well as his encouragement.

I would like to just mention the 38th and 39th chapters of Ezekiel. These two chapters tell of the catastrophic last battle -- the Battle of Armageddon. They name the nations involved, and in fact, the American Standard Version names one nation that is omitted from the Authorized King James Version, which is the version from which I have been quoting throughout this book. The nation mentioned in the American Standard Version is Rosh, or Russia. In the King James Version we have Meshech and Tubal mentioned, which scholars tell us represent Moscow and Tobolsk. I will not go into all that, for it does not come within the scope of this book.

However, remember that the Bible tells us that this nation that will attack Palestine, or Israel, will come from the "north." Also, remember that the speaker is standing in Jerusalem at the time of his prophecy, and that due north to him was Russia.

Ezekiel tells the inhabitants of Jerusalem, that "after many days thou shalt be visited; in the latter years thou shalt come into the land that is brought back from the sword, and is gathered out of many people........"

Note that Israel was not a nation at that time. Most of the Israelites were in captivity, and the others were subservient to an alien enemy. This, in itself, is a prophecy that Israel WILL be gathered back into Palestine, and WILL be a nation in its own right, and WILL be gathered together "out of many people" where they have wandered in exile for "many days." It turned out to be many years, but evidently Ezekiel did not know how long it would be.

".......Against the mountains of Israel (Ezekiel continues), which have been always waste: but it is brought forth out of the nations, and they shall dwell safely all of them. Thou (this nor-thern nation) shall ascend and come like a storm, thou shalt be like a cloud to cover the land, thou, and all thy bands, and many people with thee (satellites)."

Note "cloud to cover the land." The enemy will be airborne and probably will land in Palestine by means of parachutes.

"....To take a spoil, and to take a prey: to turn thine hand upon the desolate places that are now inhabited, and upon the people that are gathered out of the nations, which have gotten cat-tle and goods, that dwell in the midst of the land....Art thou come to take a spoil? hast thou gathered thy company to take a prey? to carry away silver and gold, to take away cattle and goods, to take a great spoil?" The Russians want the oil that is in the southern part of Palestine, but more than anything else, they want the "spoils" that lie in the Dead Sea. The Dead Sea is reckoned to contain billions of dollars worth of various minerals. It is the treasure pot of the earth.

Just read these two chapters for yourself for a picture of what is going to happen in these last days. How near is it? If I were writing on that subject, I could tell you some startling things!

THE BOOK OF DANIEL

CHAPTER 1

IN the third year of the reign of Jĕ-hoi'-ă-kim king of Judah came Nĕb-ū-chăd-nĕz'-zär king of Babylon unto Jerusalem, and besieged it.

2 And the Lord gave Jĕ-hoi'-ă-kim king of Judah into his hand, with...

and your drink: for why should he see your faces worse liking than the children which *are* of your sort? then shall ye make *me* endanger my head to the king.

11 Then said Daniel to Mĕlzar whom the prince of the eunuchs had set over Daniel, Hananiah, Mĭ'-shā-ĕl, and Ăz-ă-rī'-ăh,

12 Prove thy servants, I beseech...

TIME OF THE END?

I have mentioned earlier in this book about the three Hebrew children who were taken captive to Babylon, and because of their determination "not to defile themselves with the king's meat." They preferred to eat very simply, live simply, and continue to worship the one true God, and became foremost in the land of their captivity, favorites with the king and the people, and objects of respect all down through the centuries.

The story of Daniel being cast into the lions' den is probably the most familiar one in the Bible, with the exception of Jonah's being swallowed by a "whale." Although this story of Jonah was ascribed to by Christ himself (Matthew 12:40), I would like to add here that in the book of Jonah, "whale" is not mentioned. It says in Jonah 1:17 that "The Lord had prepared a great fish" to swallow up Jonah, and Jonah was in the belly of the fish three days and three nights. It could have been an atomic-powered submarine the Lord had prepared. Anyway, had it been an animal, the digestive juices would have digested him in three days and three nights.

But let's get back to Daniel. Daniel 6:16-24 tells the story: "Then the king commanded, and they brought Daniel, and cast him into the den of lions. Now the king spake and said unto Daniel, Thy God whom thou servest continually, he will deliver thee. And a stone was brought, and laid upon the mouth of the den; and the king sealed it with his own signet, and with the signet of his lords; that the purpose might not be changed concerning Daniel. Then the king went to his palace, and passed the night fasting: neither were instruments of music brought before him: and his sleep went from him. Then the king arose very early in the morning, and went in haste unto the den of lions. And when he came to the den, he cried with a lamentable voice unto Daniel: and the king spake and said to Daniel, O Daniel, servant of the living God, is thy God, whom thou servest continually, able to deliver thee from the lions? Then said Daniel unto the king, O king live for ever. My God has sent his angel and has shut the lions' mouths, that they have not hurt me: forasmuch as before him innocency was found in me; and also before thee, O king, have I done no hurt. Then was the king exceeding glad for him, and commanded that they should take Daniel up out of the den. So Daniel was taken up out of the den, and no matter of hurt was

There is a growing belief that the Angels described in many Biblical references were, in reality, "divine messengers" sent to Earth by some other world to teach humankind Universal laws and cosmic wisdom.

found upon him, because he believed in his God. And the king commanded, and they brought those men which had accused Daniel, and they cast them into the den of lions, them, their children, and their wives; and the lions had the mastery of them, and brake all their bones in pieces or ever they came at the bottom of the den."

Note in verse 22 that Daniel told the king, "My God hath sent his angel (and the marginal reference is "messenger") and has shut the lions' mouths, that they have not hurt me...." The visitor had to have some means of transportation to come from wherever he came from to Earth, and also, I wonder what kind of power he used to shut the lions' mouths. Did he paralyze them with some kind of ray? Or just hypnotize them?

This book has a very odd passage in it. Near the end, when God had conveyed to Daniel these mysterious prophecies, Daniel said, "And I heard, but I understood not: then said I, O, Lord, what shall be the end of these things? And he said, Go thy way, Daniel: FOR THE WORDS ARE CLOSED UP AND SEALED TILL THE TIME OF THE END."

Another reason I believe we are either nearing, or in, the time of the end of all things as we know them, is the fact that this Book of Daniel has just of recent years had commentaries written on it, and we hear sermons preached on it, but this did not used to be so.

It has been regarded as too mysterious and deep to read and understand. However, there is not a symbol used that is not repeated in the Revelation, and there is not a symbol or sign used in the Revelation that has not been used somewhere else in the Bible.

These two books are very pertinent now. Can this be the time of the end? We are certainly seeing many signs that would point to this conclusion. How about the startling "signs in the heavens?"

ZECHARIAH

CHAPTER 1

IN the eighth month, in the second year of Dă-rī'-ŭs, came the word of the Lord unto Zĕch-ă-rī'-ăh the...

man riding upon a red horse, and he stood among the myrtle trees that were in the bottom; and behind him were there red horses, speckled, and white.

9 Then said I, O my lord, what are these? And the angel that talked with me said unto me, I will shew thee what these be.

10 And the man that stood...the myrtle tr...

NAHUM

CHAPTER 1

THE burden of Nĭn'-ĕ-vĕh. The book of the vision of Nahum the Ĕl'-kō-shīte.

2 God is jealous, and the Lord revengeth...

13 For now will I break his yoke from off thee, and will burst thy bonds in sunder.

14 And the Lord hath given a commandment concerning thee...

GEOLOGISTS CONFIRM SCRIPTURE

The copy of the Bible I use for study contains an introduction to the Book of Nahum which reads, "The prophecy is one continuous strain which does not yield to analysis." The reason for this probably is that like Daniel, it is for the people who live in the time of the end. It is very definitely addressed to Gentiles, and deals with the last days.

Think on this prophecy, for instance, recorded in the second chapter of Nahum: "The chariots shall be with flaming torches in the day of his preparation, and the fir trees shall be terribly shaken. The chariots shall rage in the streets, and they shall jostle one against another in the broad ways: they shall seem like torches, they shall run like the lightnings."

This is generally taken to mean automobiles with their head-lights flaring like a torch in front of them, and of course the "broad ways" could refer to our superhighways. But the reference to the fir trees' being "shaken terribly" and the fact that they will look like lightning, makes me pause to consider. I have read of trees being shaken as UFO landed, or came near, or just plain airplanes, for that matter; and I wonder if this prophecy could not refer to both automobiles and airplanes.

Zechariah witnessed a scene between some unusual men who had evidently been on Earth for some time, and a visitor from outer space who came to get a report from them. They had been placed in Jerusalem to help the people rebuild the temple that had been ruined during their exile.

After this conference ended, evidently the men, who were rid-ing horses (Zechariah even described the horses), and the angel or messenger talked with Zechariah. The visitor told Zechariah a great many things about what was going to happen in Palestine, and Jerusalem in particular, and Zechariah was all ears -- but not sat-isfied. So the visitor either took him in a spaceship to some other part of the universe, or showed him by means of pictures, or screen, or caused him to have a vision. I am inclined to think he took Zechariah to the location, because -- well listen to Zechariah tell about it: "And he showed me Joshua (who had been dead many, many years) the high priest standing before the angel of the Lord, and Satan standing at his right hand to resist him...." This scene goes on, and Zechariah overhears a conversation that is a prophecy of the BRANCH, that is Jesus, and that is to come.

Chapter 5 of Zechariah begins thusly: "Then I turned, and lifted up mine eyes, and looked, and behold a flying roll (cigar shaped?). And he said unto me, 'What seest thou?' and I answered "I see a flying roll; the length thereof is twenty cubits, and the breadth thereof ten cubits.'"

In the 14th chapter we have a remarkable prophecy of a great earthquake: "Then shall the Lord go forth, and fight against those nations, as when he fought in the day of battle. And his feet shall stand in that day (this expression "that day" in the Old Testament almost always refers to that great day of the Lord when He shall return) upon the mount of Olives, which is before Jeru-salem on the east, and the mount of Olives shall cleave in the midst thereof toward the east and toward the west, and there shall be a very great valley; and half of the mountain shall remove to-ward the north, and half of it toward the south." Had it occurred to you that this would let the Mediterranean Sea rush in and bring water to the desert land to the East and South of Palestine?

Well, anyway, I clipped an article from <u>something</u>, dated February 24, 1957 (I am more careful now and always make sure that I have the <u>name</u> and <u>date</u>). This article goes as follows:

"Earthquakes have recently wrought damage to buildings on the Mount of Olives. The greatest earthquake, however, is yet future and will take place exactly as predicted by the Prophet Zechariah. The geological formation of the soil of the Mount of Olives is all set for the coming event. It only awaits God's appointed moment to act. Professor Bailey Willis, the Seismological expert of Leland Stanford University, made this startling statement before the British Association for the Advancement of Science: 'The region around Jerusalem is a region of potential earthquake danger. A fault line along which an earth slippage may occur at any time passes directly through the Mount of Olives!' Centuries ago, the Prophet Zechariah said, 'And His feet shall stand in that day upon the Mount of Olives ....and the Mount of Olives shall cleave in the midst thereof toward the east and toward the west, and there shall be a very great valley.' (Zechariah 14:4)"

Another point of interest in this verse (14:8): "And it shall be in that day, that living waters shall go out from Jerusalem; half of them toward the former sea, and half of them toward the hinder sea; <u>in</u> <u>summer</u> <u>and</u> <u>in</u> <u>winter</u> <u>shall</u> <u>it</u> <u>be</u>." When this great earthquake occurs that brings in <u>living</u> water (to the Dead Sea?), it will be "summer and......winter." How could such a thing be? Why, the solstice, of course.

Also in the same chapter, read this description of radiation poisoning: "Their flesh shall consume away while they stand upon their feet, and their eyes shall consume away in their holes, and their tongues shall consume away in their mouth." I guess there will be some atomic bombs used during that last great battle.

THE GOSPEL ACCORDING TO

ST. LUKE

CHAPTER 1

FORASMUCH ...

THE GOSPEL ACCORDING TO

ST. MARK

CHAPTER 1

THE GOSPEL ACCORDING TO

ST. MATTHEW

CHAPTER 1

THE book of the generation of Jesus Christ, the son of David, the son of Ab...

reth of Galilee, and was baptized of John in Jordan...

coming up the heavens like a dove

the carrying away into Babylon *are* fourteen generations; and from the carrying away into Babylon unto...

10 And the whole multitude of the people were praying without at the time of incense.

...ere appeared unto him ...the Lord standing on ...of the altar of incense. ...en Zăch-ă-rī'-ăs saw ...troubled, and fear fell

...angel said unto him, ...Zăch-ă-rī'-ăs: for thy ...rd; and thy wife Elisa-...r thee a son, and thou ...name John.

...nd thou shalt have joy and ...and many shall rejoice

THE TRANSFIGURATION

One day at Caeserea Phillipi, Jesus told His disciples that some of them standing there would not die until they had seen the Kingdom of God come with power. About one week later, on top of Mount Hermon, the tallest mountain in Palestine that stands 9166 feet high and is covered with snow the year around, an amazing thing took place.

Matthew, Mark and Luke narrate this event in practically the same words, with the exception of the fact that they use different adjectives to describe Jesus and His clothes.

Luke says that as Jesus prayed, His countenance changed, or was altered, "and his raiment was white and glistening." Matthew says that Jesus was "transfigured before them. And his raiment became shining exceeding white as snow; so as no fuller on earth can white them." In other words, Jesus shone so that it was as though they were looking into the sun to look at Him. We are told that in that place where we will live eternally, we shall be clothed with light.

When Moses came down from off the top of Mount Sinai when he had received the Ten Commandments from God, he had this same shining radiant appearance. The people could not bear to look at him. What caused this incandescence?

Let's read on: "And there appeared unto them Elijah with Moses: and they were talking with Jesus (Mark)." Luke says, "And, behold, there talked with him two men, which were Moses and Elijah."

Now, we remember that Elijah left this earth without experiencing death. He was caught away in a "fiery chariot." Elisha saw him leave. Now it seems that Elijah has made a round trip --- somewhere --- by spaceship. Here he is back on Mount Hermon, where he had visited many times in his lifetime most probably.

Moses, too, is here. Moses died. Nobody knew just when or

where. He had gotten real old, and would sit on the mountainside
and look over into the promised land of Canaan, and wish that somehow he could hasten the Israelites along so they could make it during his lifetime. But God told him that because of his disobedience
he could not go into the Holy Land. He died somewhere up on Mount
Nebo, and God Himself buried him. But death is not the end, thank
God! Here we have Moses, himself shining like a neon light, in the
Promised Land, talking with Elijah and Jesus. The Bible says that
the three disciples, Peter, James and John, saw the glory of all
three of these men.

What were they talking about? Again, Luke: "Who appeared in
glory and spake of his decease which he should accomplish at Jerusalem." They spake of His (Jesus') death and resurrection. In
the Book of Acts we are told how more than 500 disciples saw Jesus
ascend into heaven, or rather, "...a cloud received Him from their
sight." Do you suppose that at this time, here on Mount Hermon,
they made arrangements for taking Jesus back to His heavenly home
after His resurrection? We know Jesus longed for this glorious
home because one day when He was praying He mentioned "The glory
that was mine before the world was."

Elijah and Moses didn't just drift through the atmosphere,
or rather lack of it, in space, because all three accounts of this
amazing incident tell us that, "behold, a bright cloud overshadowed
them: and behold a voice out of the cloud, which said, This is my
beloved Son, in whom I am well pleased; hear ye him."

This conveyance was large enough to overshadow them, six men
on top of the mountain. Either it was putting out a vapor cloud to
cut down on the brilliance of the vehicle, or it was grey like a
cloud. It was noteworthy, enough so that all three of the writers
mention it. At a time like this, when two men who had been gone
from Earth for hundreds of years, and when Jesus was so transfigured
before them that they could not keep their eyes open because of the
light, with all these amazing things happening, they mention this
large "cloud" hovering over them and overshadowing them.

But more: there was at least one other person aboard that
space ship that day. While this strange conference was in progress
"Behold, a voice out of the cloud, which said, This is my beloved
Son, in whom I am well pleased; hear ye him." God himself added
His word of approval to Jesus and His work. You know, that is
God's opinion of Jesus: "I am well pleased." Sometimes we think
very lightly of Jesus, and even take His holy name in vain, and
worse yet, even use His name profanely. But the God of all the
universe is well pleased with Him. Think about it.

Well, Peter, James and John certainly saw the "power" part of
the Kingdom of God, didn't they? Jesus told them they would. I
can't imagine any demonstration of power that would equal a huge
spaceship.

They never forgot it, either. Later, Peter, in his second

epistle, says, "For we have not followed cunningly devised fables, when we made known unto you the power and coming of our Lord Jesus Christ, but were eyewitnesses of his majesty. For he received from God the Father honour and glory, when there came such a voice to him from the excellent glory, This is my beloved Son, in whom I am well pleased. And this voice which came from heaven we heard, when we were with him in the holy mount."

THE
REVELATION
OF ST. JOHN THE DIVINE

CHAPTER 1

THE Revelation of Jesus Christ, which God gave unto him, to shew unto his servants things which must ... come to ...

called Patmos, for the word of God, and for the testimony of Jesus Christ.
10 I was in the Spirit on the Lord's day, and heard ... me a great ...

A CORNER OF HEAVEN

Aged John the Beloved, exiled on Patmos, had quite an experience. He had been put on a little coral island out in the ocean where, no doubt, his persecutors thought that he would soon die. There was no water, no food, no vegetation. But Sunday rolled around, and being Christian, John said to himself, "I'm going to church." Revelation 1:10: "I was in the Spirit on the Lord's day."

Incidentally, I want to preach a little sermon here. We dress our bodies to go to church, but we rarely ever prepare our spirits to meet God. We should meditate upon what it means to worship. Think of it -- coming into the presence of God! Expect God to come into our presence! That's worship. We would rather enjoy our Beauty Rest mattresses, read the paper, enjoy a leisurely breakfast, on the Lord's day, than to get ourselves out and go to church. "I was in the Spirit on the Lord's day."

Well, God came to church that day, as He does every time a truly worshipping soul does, and He said to John, "Come up hither, I want to show you something, and I want you to write it down so coming generations will know something of what goes on in heaven." Had John looked around him at his circumstances, he could have written what he saw in one word -- "Nothing."

God never tells us to do something that He does not provide the means of our accomplishing. So, when He invited John to "Come up hither," He sent a conveyance and just opened up a corner of heaven and John sailed in! And what he saw! Well, just read the Book.

In the first chapter of the Revelation, and in the 7th verse, John says, "Behold, he cometh with clouds; and every eye shall see him and they also which pierced him; and all kindreds of the earth shall wail because of him. Even so, Amen."

As I mentioned before, it seems that our relationship to God determines our ability to see the wonderful conveyances (as well as many spiritual truths) of God, but in the verse quoted above we find that there will be a time when "every eye shall see him and they also which pierced him." But when they see Him on this particular occasion they will be wailing because of Him, because at this time He will be coming in judgment.

IN THE END A "GOLDEN AGE" WILL EMERGE FROM THE DESTRUCTION

EPILOGUE

As I end this study of flying saucers and related phenomena in the Bible, I would like to add that the Word of God is very precious to me, and that I believe it -- every bit of it -- from the stately "In the beginning...." to the last "Amen."

I also want to add that I am very mindful of the warning given in the very last verses of the Bible: "If any man shall add unto these things, God shall add unto him the plagues that are written in this book: And if any man shall take away from the words of the book of this prophecy, God shall take away his part out of the book of life, and out of the holy city, and from the things which are written in this book."

I do not want to "add to" whatever message God has for us in His Word, and if you will note, in quoting passages from the Bible, I have not merely lifted a phrase and isolated it to make it mean anything I wanted it to. In all instances I have quoted the entire context, or if not, because of length, I have urged the reader to read these passages. While I do not want to "add to" the Word of God, neither do I want to "take away" from it, and if some of these interpretations I have advanced are new to you, that does not necessarily mean they are not right. However, I am not dogmatic about anything I have said, but I do believe it. I want all God has for me -- both in His Word, and in spiritual experience -- in this world and in the next.

In the second chapter of First Corinthians we have these thrilling words: "But as it is written, Eye hath not seen, nor ear heard, neither have entered into the heart of man, the things which God has prepared for them that love him. But God hath revealed them unto us by his Spirit; for the Spirit searcheth all things, yea, the deep things of God.......But the natural man receiveth not the things of the Spirit of God: for they are foolishness unto him: neither can he know them, because they are spiritually discerned."

As a word of personal testimony, I want to say that I do love the Lord with all my heart; my most intense desire is to serve Him in a manner that is pleasing to Him, and to lead others into this glorious freedom of the Spirit.

I hope and pray that you will have enjoyed reading this, and that it will give you a desire to read the Bible more and with greater interest, that it will inspire you to follow more closely to the Savior so that He can whisper His choicest secrets to you, and that you will be able to say with John the Beloved, "Even so, come, Lord Jesus."

REV. VIRGINIA F. BRASINGTON

ABDUCTIONS IN LIGHT OF HOLY SCRIPTURES

By Sean Casteel

EDITOR'S NOTE: In recent years we have seen a new UFO-related phenomenon emerge, the abduction of humans by the occupants of these swirling, whirling objects. The majority of cosmic kidnappings do not take place on isolated roads in the dead of night (though some like the classic case of Betty and Barney Hill certainly do), but in the homes of unsuspecting folks who more often than not have no forewarning that they are about to come face-to-face with something that could either be from Heaven or Hell. And so what is the connection between these hundreds–possibly thousands of abductions–and the sacred scriptures of the Bible? Noted scholar and author Sean Casteel has been hot on the trail of the abductees and has some startling thoughts and conclusions to offer which might be of value to students of the Bible.

"I sat with my legs partly bent and my hands in my lap. Although I cannot recall this in any detail, I may have been leaning against something. I was still absent sensation. Across the depression to my left there was a small individual whom I could see only out of the corner of my eye. This person was wearing a gray-tan body suit and sitting on the ground with knees drawn up and hands clasped around them. There were two dark eyeholes and a round mouth hole. I had the impression of a face mask.

"I felt that I was under the exact and detailed control of whomever had me. I could not move my head, or my hands, or any part of my body save my eyes. Immediately on my right was another figure, this one invisible except for an occasional flash of movement. This person was working at something that seemed to have to do with the right side of my head. It wore dark-blue overalls and was extremely fast.

"The next thing I knew, I was sitting in a messy round room...The fear was so powerful that it seemed to make my personality completely evaporate. This was not a theoretical or even a mental experience, but something profoundly physical . . . . I was so scared that my memories are indistinct and covered by amnesia. Even as I write this, I am aware that a great deal more happened. I just can't get to it."

– **Whitley Streiber,** *Communion, A True Story*, **1987**

● ● ●

FLYING SAUCERS IN THE HOLY BIBLE

"Suddenly, the electric lights began to flicker hesitantly and then blinked out, throwing the house into darkness and confusion and sending frightened children scurrying into the kitchen to find their mother. Almost at the same time, the family saw a curious pink light shining through the kitchen window. Ten years later, under hypnosis, Betty and Becky Andreasson would describe the scene as follows:

Betty: Suddenly the lights were off, and we wondered, what was it? And we looked over and there was a . . . by the window, the small kitchen window . . . I can see like a light, sort of pink right now. And now the light is getting brighter. It's reddish-orange, and it's pulsating. I said to the children, 'Be quiet, and quick, get in the living room, and whatever it is will go away.' It seemed like the whole house had a vacuum over it. Like stillness all around, like stillness.

Becky: The next thing I knew, Mom was going, 'Shhh! Be quiet!' There's some huge pulsating glow that was out in the kitchen. It was outside. Like a big glow!
"When the bright light first flashed through the kitchen window, Becky had returned into the living room in response to her mother's commands. Looking down the hallway into the kitchen, she noticed a dark silhouetted shape bobbing in front of the light source shining through the kitchen window. Then, everything went black. At that same moment, Becky, her grandfather, and all family members except Betty found themselves unable to move, unaware of anything else.

Betty: There's some . . . the lights are back on now and, ah, there are beings standing there and they're talking with me, but not with their mouths. They've got big heads. They came through the door. They came in like follow-the-leader. They are starting to come through the door now. Right through the wood, one right after the other. It's amazing. Coming through. And I stood back a little. Was it real? And they are coming, one after another...Now they are all inside. I thought, how did they ever do that? How did they get in here like that? I'm thinking they must be angels, because Jesus was able to walk through doors and walls and walk on water. Must be angels. . . And Scriptures keep coming into my mind where it says, 'Entertain the stranger, for it may be angels unaware.'"

--**Raymond Fowler**, *The Andreasson Affair*, 1979

•   •   •

70

FLYING SAUCERS IN THE HOLY BIBLE

"There was an oval-shaped object hovering over the top of the apartment building two or three blocks up from where we were sitting. We didn't know where it came from, it happened too fast. Its lights turned from a bright reddish-orange to a whitish-blue coming out of the bottom of it. There on the side of the craft near the top of it, just above the protruding saucer ledge, I could see horizontal, rectangular-shaped windows around the object. At the very edge of the object, on the edge of the protruding saucer ledge, were green rotating lights rotating round and round while the craft stood still, just hovering off of the building. It moved out away from the building and lowered itself to the apartment window below, about two windows down. I yelled for my partner sitting behind the wheel of the car. He was astonished as I was. Yes, it was like science fiction objects that we used to laugh at many years ago on TV . . . .

"We wanted to get out of the car to see what we could do. What were we going to do? Shoot at it? We stayed in the car and the worst happened. A little girl or woman wearing a full white gown sailed out of the window in a fetal position. Linda was there now in a standing position in midair in this beam of light. She looked like an angel or a Christmas tree doll. Then the lights underneath the object dimmed and we directed ourselves toward Linda.

"With my binoculars I could see three of the ugliest creatures I ever saw. I don't know what they were. They weren't human. Their heads were all out of proportion. Very large heads with no hair. The eyes were very large, very large eyes. I don't know what color they were, maybe white. Very thin, too thin, smaller than Linda in height. One of them was standing above her in midair and two were beneath her. Those buggers were escorting her into the craft. They were completely in charge, all right . . . . She was gone, they took her away." [A partial transcript of a recording made by "Richard," the pseudonym of a security guard who was one of the eyewitnesses to Linda Cortile's abduction in November of 1989.]

--Budd Hopkins, *Witnessed*: *The True Story of the Brooklyn Bridge Abductions*, **1996**

● ● ●

According to Dr. John Mack, Harvard psychiatrist and author of two essential books on abduction, ***Abduction*** (1994) and ***Passport To The Cosmos*** (1999), one of the most common reactions a person has to becoming aware of their abduction experiences is something he labeled "ontological shock." The sudden jolt to the system of learning there is another reality never before dreamed of by the abductee causes a dramatic shift in consciousness, and an entirely new realm of experience must be assimilated.

71

FLYING SAUCERS IN THE HOLY BIBLE

That assimilation process, however, is often slow and tortuous. And among the many subjects the abductee is forced to think differently about, religion stands out as one of the major problem areas. An abductee must often ask, "How did God let this happen to me?" or any of a number of theological and philosophical questions that bombard the mind as the person begins to try to navigate between the abduction experience and what was once "normal" reality.

When I began to take an interest in the UFO phenomenon, as a Christian and a journalist, the thing I was most curious about was the moral quality of the aliens, whether we were dealing with proverbial soul-stealing demons or soul-healing angels in the increasingly numerous accounts of sightings and abductions. The answers I got were as vague and as inconclusive as the answers to most of the other aspects of the phenomenon. Like every other "unknown," the moral nature of the UFO occupants was open to any number of contradictory and unsatisfying conclusions.

Beginning in the spring of 1989, I interviewed some of the famous researchers and witnesses, such as Raymond Fowler, Budd Hopkins, Betty Andreasson Luca and Whitley Strieber, among many others. In each case, at some point, I asked for their moral and religious perspectives on their research and experiences. The interviewees responded with a wide range of moral responses, running the gamut from reluctant agnosticism to heartfelt belief in the righteousness of the abducting aliens.

RAYMOND FOWLER

Raymond Fowler is a veteran UFO researcher and the author of numerous books on the subject of alien abduction. He served with the US Air Force as a Security Officer and spent twenty-five years with GTE Government Systems where he worked as Task Manager and Senior Planner for several major weapons systems, including the Minuteman and MX missiles. As a director of investigations for the Mutual UFO Network, he appeared frequently on such television programs as Good Morning America, Unsolved Mysteries, and Sightings.

Fowler is perhaps best known for his five-part series on abductee Betty Andreasson Luca, which began in 1979 with *The Andreasson Affair*, and was followed by *The Andreasson Affair Phase Two* (1982), *The Watchers* (1990), *The Watchers II* (1995) and *The Andreasson Legacy* (1997).   In an interview I conducted with Fowler in 1991, he said, "I started officially investigating the UFO phenomenon in 1963. I have now found that the phenomenon has been investigating me since 1938!"

FLYING SAUCERS IN THE HOLY BIBLE

Fowler's discovery that he was also an abductee was first revealed in *The Watchers*, which was the above mentioned third installment of the complex research into Betty Andreasson Luca and her long history of contact with extraterrestrials. Being on both sides of the subject, as a researcher and an experiencer, gives Fowler a uniquely well-informed perspective on the subject.

I asked Fowler the following: You and Betty are both Christians who feel these experiences have a religious overtone. Do prophecies of the Apocalypse enter your thinking about the aliens? Do you think the world, as we know it today, is doomed by the things the aliens are said to warn us against, like nuclear war or ecological disaster?

"Betty certainly believes," Fowler began, "that her experiences are angelic in nature, and that they correspond to her Christian belief system, which would include prophecies of the Apocalypse and the Second Coming of Christ. As Christians, both of us believe that Jesus Christ is our only hope. I would like to believe that such a connection exists and that past and present UFO manifestations in our history have a direct connection with the Judeo-Christian tradition. However, all one can really say for sure is that what is being seen today was also seen in Biblical times, only it would have been interpreted within a religious context, not a scientific one.

Conversely, if some of the phenomena reported in Biblical accounts were reported today, they would be placed in a UFO context."

FOWLER'S CHRISTIAN STRUGGLE

In another interview I did with Fowler in 1997, he spoke movingly about his struggle to balance his abduction experiences with his Christian beliefs.

"On the objective side of my faith," he said, "there has been an ever-growing tension between my theological beliefs and my theoretical hypotheses about the origin and meaning behind the UFO phenomenon and my own apparent abductions. My former pastor, whose wife had a Close Encounter experience of the First Kind [sighting a ship], once asked me how I integrated my UFO research and experiences with my Christian faith. I replied that at the present time I had no choice but to 'compartmentalize' them.

"In short," he continued, "I find myself living a double life as a UFO researcher/experiencer on the one hand and a devoted Christian on the other while trying to erect a harmonious bridge between the two. Thus I find myself living with a continual tension between two worlds, both of which are very real to me."

Fowler told the story of how he had experienced an emotion he called "Unconditional Love" in both a Christian context and an alien one, and that they seemed to be related—at least coincidentally. The story began when Fowler was still in adolescence.

"It was on the evening of May 19, 1950," he said. "Several weeks earlier, I had befriended a boy from a broken home who was going to be placed in a state institution for the homeless. I had persuaded my parents to let him live with us. He shared my room. He and his friends were Christians, and over those weeks they shared their faith with me.

"On the night in question," he went on, "unknown to my roommate at the time, while lying in bed, I privately received Christ into my life. When doing so, I experienced an inner feeling of pure, unconditional love as an outside Presence entered and filled my being. As this was happening to me, my roommate exclaimed that there was a bright light hovering over the house. But I paid little attention to what he said because of what was happening to me experientially. It was only years later, when he visited me again and again told me about the bright light that we both wondered if it was UFO-related. A check of astronomical records revealed no such bright object in the sky on that date and time."

That unusual sensation of unconditional love has happened to Fowler on more than one occasion.

"I have felt this identical feeling of unconditional love," he said, "envelop me on a number of occasions, including during what seem to have been UFO abductions. For example, I felt it as a child when awakened by a lady enveloped in light who floated me through my bedroom window up a beam of light to some lights in the sky. So from the very beginning, and throughout my Christian walk of life, there seems to be at least a subjective, mystical-like, coincidental connection between my UFO and Christian-related experiences."

So again I asked if Fowler's UFO research and experiences had affected his religious beliefs.

"Sure they have," he said, "and hopefully, in the long run, for the good—although I am prepared to accept the bad as well. On the one hand, I continue to attend church, sing in the choir, teach adult Sunday school and attempt with God's help to live a good Christian life.

FLYING SAUCERS IN THE HOLY BIBLE

On the other hand, I continue to live in tension as I attempt to construct a bridge between two sometimes seemingly opposing but true experiences—the double life of a Christian believer and UFO experiencer."

BETTY ANDREASSON LUCA

Betty Andreasson Luca was born in Fitchburg, Mass. in 1937, to devoutly Pentecostal Christian parents. She married James Andreasson, and the couple became the parents of seven children. Betty and James divorced, and she later married Bob Luca, who was also an alien abductee.

Betty's first recalled abduction experience is partially recounted at the beginning of this chapter. The events took place in the family house in South Ashburnham, Massachusetts, in 1967. It was the first of many experiences that Betty would recall only after the fact and while under hypnosis. Raymond Fowler helped lead her through her regressive hypnosis sessions and offered moral support and educated insight as well as writing the books on her continuing story mentioned earlier.

Luca, who began working with Fowler to finally uncover her abduction experiences more than twenty-five years ago, seems not to suffer from the same lingering doubt as Fowler or to view her contact with aliens as in some way diametrically opposed to her Christian beliefs.

I first interviewed Luca in 1991, a few months after I had spoken to Fowler. Luca was of particular interest to me because she was an abductee who unflinchingly believed in the religious aspect of her contacts, and that she had been contacted by angels, a leap of faith many abductees were unable to make.

"I believe that UFO contacts are of an angelic nature," Luca said, "whether good or bad, and I base this statement primarily on my faith and knowledge acquired during personal encounters. Regardless of whether it is God's angels or lost, fallen angels, we humans are the battleground or territory either side wishes to gain. My encounters with benevolent beings have strengthened my faith in the reality of the seldom-seen world of the government of God. His messengers have been sent to do His will, and although I have seen and heard yet not always understood, I can rest in His promises and faith."

A few years later, when I spoke to Luca again, her faith remained much the same.

FLYING SAUCERS IN THE HOLY BIBLE

"My UFO encounters with extraterrestrials," she said, "which I still believe to be Angels or Messengers, have helped me to mature as a child of God. My Christian faith is of the utmost importance to me, and I believe it has occasionally given me access to a realm rarely seen by physical eyes. And yet this God-given rite of passage can exist for everyone, for the Creator is not a respecter of persons. His love for everyone is unconditional and encompasses all.

"I've chosen the Old and New Testament," she continued, "as my road map, and embraced with all my heart the humble being who gave his all for me. He loved us more than life. When he died on a cross and rose to his celestial abode, his child began to grow inside each believer from the seeds of his Word. His child in us increases as we decrease. After complete surrender to Christ, the beginning of wisdom grew.

"It was not long before extraterrestrial visitation began," she said. "While immersed in a benign celestial world filled with mystery, the angelic host began to reveal themselves little by little."

Such a cheerful outlook stands in marked contrast to the trauma and terror reported by most abductees. But Luca had an answer for those critical voices as well.

"I cannot express enough," she said, "the real need to be grounded in faith when exposed to the spiritual world of UFOs. For once there, you will experience what eyes have not seen and ears have not heard. For the unprepared, it can be a world of sheer terror. For when man neglects to know himself and his Maker, it leaves him open to fear."

Luca acknowledged that a lot of her views are not shared by some.

"Unfortunately," she said, "many who worship today account the angels or extraterrestrials to be demons and evil spirits. But God is the same yesterday, today and tomorrow. As in the days of yesteryear, when He spoke to Moses, Jacob, Joseph and David, to Matthew, Mark, Luke and John – He'll speak to us today through His Son, The Christ, the Spirit, and The Watchers [a term Fowler and Luca sometimes use for aliens that is taken from Old Testament scriptures], and tomorrow he will be the same God for generations to come."

For Luca, alien abduction is not something God helps her endure, it is the experience of union with God Himself.

FLYING SAUCERS IN THE HOLY BIBLE

"My faith is as strong as the Rock I stand on," she said. "And because I've experienced a deep walk and been privy to personal extraterrestrial encounters, I am blessed."

I also asked Luca the following question: Does the idea of abduction match up with the Christian idea of "Rapture" in your mind? Is it meaningful to you to think of the current activities of the aliens as possibly having something to do with the prophecies of the Apocalypse?

"Quite possibly," Luca replied. "There is scripture to support the idea. In the Book of Luke 17: 34-36, Christ says, 'In that night, there shall be two men in one bed. One shall be taken, and the other shall be left. Two women shall be grinding together. The one shall be taken, and the other left. Two men shall be in the fields, and one shall be taken, and the other left.'

"Further evidence," she continued, "that may support the Rapture is verses 30 and 31.

'Even thus shall it be in the day when the Son of Man shall be revealed. In that day, he which shall be upon the housetop and his stuff in the house, let him not come down to take it away. And he that is in the field, let him likewise not return back.'

"Doesn't it sound familiar?" she asked. "Of course most Christians believe it will be one swoop of believers, starting first with those who are in the grave and have died in faith, and those believers that remain will be caught up in the air."

So from two Christian believers come answers that rest firmly on their bedrock of ultimate faith. I know I am not alone in being consoled by their heavenly interpretation of what could otherwise be a tremendously frightening experience with no redeeming moral value at all.

It is wise to be thankful for small mercies, and perhaps the mercy implied in this understanding of the abduction experience will grow as the days, months and years go on.

WHITLEY STRIEBER

Whitley Strieber is perhaps the most famous of all the abductees who have put their experiences down on paper. His hugely successful first book on the subject, *Communion*, was number one on the bestseller lists in 1987 for several weeks. He also published many

77

FLYING SAUCERS IN THE HOLY BIBLE

sequels, including *Transformation* (1988), *Breakthrough* (1995), *The Secret School* (1997), *The Communion Letters* (1997) and *Confirmation* (1998). Strieber's struggle to come to grips with aliens he called "The Visitors" has been arduous but rewarding, not only for himself and his family, but for millions of others who have had similar events happen in their lives.

Strieber began his career as a writer of horror fiction, and authored, among many others, the hit novels *The Wolfen* and *The Hunger*, both of which were made into successful movies. When *Communion* made its initial appearance as a bestseller, it was widely suggested that Strieber had used his skills as a horror novelist to concoct simply another scary story, and had labeled it as "true" only to boost the book's sales. For Strieber, though, it was the beginning of a new life in which his alien abduction experiences were only too real.

When I asked Strieber for his views on the moral aspects of alien abduction at our very first meeting in 1989, he began by saying, "I see the Visitor experience as being very similar to experiences which have happened to many other people in the past, ranging from St. Paul's unusual experience on the road to Damascus, to the apparitions of Fatima. I can really see my experiences as being in line with historical encounters of supposed spirits, demons and angels. My experiences run the full gamut of all that."

When I interviewed Strieber again, in June of 1993, he had changed his religious interpretation to a rather negative one.

"I've never encountered anything," he said, "that was pleasant or angelic in any way. It's always been very difficult and very scary and, as often as not, dangerous. I've come away from this experience convinced of one thing: if there aren't any demons out there, there might as well be because these guys are indistinguishable from demons. To see them, to look into their eyes, is to be less, forever. It hurts you, takes from you forever because then you know it really exists. And that makes you less."

At this point, I was a little discouraged myself. But Strieber managed to leave a little room for hope regarding his interpretation of his friend Betty Andreasson Luca.

"The number of us who are so spiritually superb as Betty," he said, "who can really make this encounter fly, is tiny. Most of us are down in the muck struggling with it. That's why Betty is such an inspiration to me. When I was at the depths of my depression, one of the things I did was read Betty's interviews and listen to her tapes, just to hear the sound of her voice. I would also look at drawings she sent me and it helped a lot. Betty's experiences are the thing you grab onto while you're sinking."

In fairness to Strieber, he resists launching into a black versus white moral debate.

"I don't believe," he said, "in dichotomies of black and white, good and evil. It isn't the way life works and it isn't the way this experience works. It can be a very rough experience, there's no doubt about it. It is rarely a beautiful experience, in the sentimental sense of 'sweetness and light.' It is always, however, if you wish it to be, a useful experience in terms of growth of knowledge, character and understanding. But it can be devastating, which it has been for me at times, because of its sheer power and the tremendously difficult experience of facing an enigma so volatile.

"This is the most complex experience," he continued, "that anyone has ever had. The totality of the encounter experience is incredibly complex. It is shaded with dozens of different layers of meaning. To try and make it into something black and white or to divide people according to this black and white issue of whether the so-called aliens are good or bad is to fail to even begin to see what's going on. As far as I'm concerned, the UFO community, which revolves around this black or white interpretation, literally has no idea what's going on. They haven't even begun."

I interviewed Strieber again a few years later and asked him if his experiences had affected his religious beliefs any differently since we last discussed the subject.

"There's never been much of a connection," he said. "No matter what my religious beliefs at any given time may or may not have been, the close encounter experience simply doesn't affect them. I have been many different things in my life. As a child, I was a Catholic. When I grew up, I joined the Gurdjieff Foundation [where I studied meditation] and became very interested in 'waking up' and not so interested in my Catholic background. I went through a period of being very interested in paganism. I returned to Catholicism again, and now I am sort of less interested in it. There are elements of Catholicism, such as the belief in the Resurrection, that I'm having a lot of trouble with. But none of this has anything to do with my close encounter experiences."

Strieber said the religious changes he has gone through are "typical of anyone who has a religious life at all and is concerned with the welfare of their soul."

FLYING SAUCERS IN THE HOLY BIBLE

But still he has reservations.

"I don't even know if I have a soul," he said. "I've never been sure about that. I think so, and I think so because I have a lot of evidence that suggests that something exists that is more than just the physical body. But whether that persists after the death of the body, I haven't the faintest idea."

While he professes not to know, Strieber also resists the word "agnostic."

"The word 'agnostic' is such a copout," he said. "I hate it. I'm actively searching, let's put it that way. As I say, the close encounter experience doesn't seem to be too related to religion. The Visitors never seemed to indicate any religious beliefs. They don't fit into any religious cosmology."

Strieber said that when people attempt to match the experience to religious tradition, they do so for lack of a better way to describe the aliens.

"To me," he said, "they're not demons or angels. I think the main problem that we have right now is that we can't describe them. And because we can't describe them, we keep trying to fit them into old descriptions that don't necessarily fit."

LINDA CORTILE

Linda Cortile (a pseudonym) is the focal point of the story Budd Hopkins tells in his 1996 book *Witnessed: The True Story of the Brooklyn Bridge UFO Abductions*. The New York City housewife was abducted by aliens from her high-rise apartment in full view of several witnesses, hence the book's title. Her experience was hailed as "The Case of the Century" at the time, mainly because of all the objective proof, at least in terms of eyewitnesses, that was available to Hopkins as a researcher when he began to investigate Cortile's claims.

Like Strieber, Cortile was also raised as a Catholic.

"I've always had my faith," she said. "I was never an ultra-religious person, but I am a Roman Catholic. And I've always loved my religion."

Cortile said that God's role in her abduction experiences was to help her endure them.

FLYING SAUCERS IN THE HOLY BIBLE

"I couldn't believe I pulled through it," she said, "and am presently mentally stable. I really don't know where that strength came from. It had to come from God. And so my faith is stronger as far as religion is concerned."

Neither was it God's will that she was chosen to be an abductee.

"I don't believe God did this to me," she said. "It's just something that happened. And what had happened to me as far as aliens are concerned is as natural as life, death, and love. God gave me the strength to go through it.

"However, I don't believe religion has anything to do with the aliens," she continued. "The only religious aspect of it that I can see is that God created them, too. But I don't believe he goes around abducting people."

BUDD HOPKINS

UFO abduction researcher Budd Hopkins, the aforementioned author of *Witnessed*, has also written two other classics on alien abduction, *Missing Time* (1981) and *Intruders* (1987). Hopkins has always been a trailblazer in the field of abduction research. He was the first to uncover the alien genetic experiments that have since come to be regarded as perhaps the true purpose behind the abduction experience. He also coined the term "screen memory" to describe how the process of the amnesia imposed by the aliens works to obscure the abductees' recollection of their experience.

His answers to my questions regarding good versus evil were a little different. Hopkins replied with what I considered a rather skillful analogy.

"Is Exxon a malevolent company, or a benign, helpful, wonderful company?" he asked. "First, you start with the oil spill—there's no arguing with the oil spill. But the oil spill doesn't let you know Exxon's intentions or its moral character, its nature. One of the things I try very hard to do in both Intruders and Missing Time is to avoid a kind of final statement as to the nature of the UFO occupants.

"I can understand the impulse of a Whitley Strieber or a Dr. Leo Sprinkle [Sprinkle is a Wyoming UFO researcher who advocates the aliens as benevolent], or of other people who believe that there's some kind of wonderful understanding, like God loves us or something. Everybody likes to believe that even though Mommy and Daddy are wonderful and nice,

BUDD HOPKINS

somewhere out there in the sky there's somebody even nicer who really does love us and understand us. And I can understand why somebody would want this concept to be true, and as a matter of fact, I would like it to be true. Who the heck wouldn't? But that is just not what is going on. Unfortunately, there is a gap of understanding which is separate from the idea of an innate malevolence or anything of that sort."

When I asked Hopkins if there was some degree of masochism involved in these abduction experiences, he replied, "In some cases there's something of that, too. But the problem is this: if someone hurts you in some context or says something stupid to hurt your feelings, if you're normal you say to yourself something like, 'I know this person and he's ordinarily okay, and I don't know why he did this. But I don't like that aspect of him.' You don't just think all of a sudden, 'I now believe that person is a demon.' Should that same person take you out to dinner and behave very civilly toward you, you don't suddenly think, 'I thought he was just a nice, interesting person, but now I regard him as a god.' You don't translate the nature of the person just because of how you feel at the moment that he's treated you. Doing so is really to act as a child. The issue of what the UFO occupants are actually doing to us, physically and psychologically, is an issue we can address rationally and with some certainty. The innate nature of the aliens, physically, psychologically and ethically is quite another issue, and is presently unknowable."

KATHARINA WILSON

I also spoke to abductee Katharina Wilson, the author of *The Alien Jigsaw* (1995). Wilson self-published her book about her abduction experiences and managed to sell out her first printing, a testimony to the intriguing nature of the story she had to tell. Like many abductees, she comes away from the experience with a great deal of anger directed at the aliens, but she also manages to maintain an admirable level of objectivity as she struggles through whatever transformation she has been selected for.

For Wilson, church attendance began in childhood but lost its luster after she became aware she was an abductee.

"I went to church every Sunday until I was eighteen years old," Wilson said. "I don't remember ever leaving church feeling good about myself or life in general. I was made to feel guilty rather than hopeful or uplifted. I never understood that, but I knew I didn't like it."

Wilson was only 21-years-old when the pivotal experience of seeing an unearthly yellow light appear in her bedroom made her doubt her sanity. She had begun attending a fundamentalist church at around the same time.

"After some bizarre conversations about whether this light was from God or Satan," she said, "and after learning about some of the people I was involved with, I realized these people were dangerous. As I look back on that time, with their attempts at trying to get me to quit college in my senior year and to disown my family and friends, I realize it was more of a cult than anything."

Wilson said that ultimately there is not much difference between the aliens and organized religion.

"Both seem to use a level of manipulation," she said, "to obtain their desired result. Churches will instill fear and guilt to obtain your money. Aliens instill fear and guilt to obtain your Will."

Like Cortile, Wilson credits God with helping her endure the trauma of abduction.

"I think living under such extreme pressures," she said, "has forced me to look to my inner strengths for survival. When my inner strength is exhausted, I am forced to reach out to that which created me: God. I am slowly gaining strength from God. I believe that God is real and that God cares."

Wilson also feels there are ways to resist an abduction experience when it is happening and to fight off the abductors using such techniques as "mental struggle," "righteous anger," and "protective rage," methods originally developed by abduction researcher Ann Druffel. In other words, to visual images and learn attitudes that drive the aliens away.

"It is important to me to add that I do not believe these techniques will work," she said, "if there is even one molecule in your body that still wants to participate even if it's for the learning experience or for curiosity's sake. Unless every fiber in your body 'believes' you really want them out of your life, they will know it and they will come back."

Wilson also feels God offers help with the resistance process.

"Today," she said, "when I feel I may be curious about them, I concentrate on God, or the Creative Force, what ever you want to call it, and I say, 'If I need answers — or if I need the truth about the phenomenon—it will come from God, not aliens.' It's a way to remind myself and the aliens that I am aware of the enormous manipulative abilities they have."

Still there is an upside to Wilson's experiences which involves the notion of "Spirituality."

"Perhaps it is that which organized religion is so severely lacking," she said. "The teaching of Spirituality, which has helped me more than anything. In some cases, my involvement with certain aliens has taken me in to the Spiritual Realm and what I believe to be other dimensions or realities. Unlike most people on our planet, I know these realms exist. Spirituality is what is important, not religion."

PROPHECIES GIVEN TO WILSON

The abduction experience often carries with it a deep sense of responsibility. Wilson talked more about visions of the future she has received.

"Like many abductees," Wilson said, "I feel a great weight upon me, as if I am preparing for an important event to take place. I also feel as if I am, in part, responsible for something very important. I want to make it very clear that I do not feel special because of my experiences. Quite the contrary. I feel an enormous burden because of these experiences, and rather than feeling I've been 'chosen,' I feel as if it is my duty or my assignment to help educate people about this phenomenon."

That burdensome sense of responsibility also includes receiving frightening visions of the Earth's future and mankind's own powerlessness in the face of global nuclear and environmental disaster.

"In early 1995," Wilson said, "I had a vision of nuclear war that I documented in an unpublished paper called '*Curious Correlations*.' The vision showed that China will attack both Russia and the United States with nuclear weapons. They will be carried by red, high performance jets belonging to the Chinese military. Nuclear weapons and oil are going to be the main 'tools' of this war.

"How do I feel about visions such as these?" Wilson continued. "First, I have no idea why I'm receiving information such as this, unless I'm supposed to share it with others. It does me no personal good to have to live with this knowledge, if that is indeed what it is.

Second, I don't want anything like this to occur, and my life isn't so boring that I would create something like this to make it more interesting. As to the 'reality' of these visions, I can only describe them as being absolutely 'powerful.' When you see these events unfolding before you, at that moment, you have no choice but to believe them."

I asked her if she had received any other visions about the future of mankind.

"I was given a vision of 'humanity,'" she replied. "'Humanity' was standing in line inside a mall at a burger joint, content with their minimum wage jobs. They weren't striving for anything more in life. They weren't trying to educate themselves. They weren't trying to make a positive difference. They were satisfied. A female Being with dark skin and funny looking glasses was standing next to me. She was telepathically tuning into my thoughts. I said to her, 'I can't believe they're satisfied with this. Eating animals and existing to work.' The female telepathically replied, matter-of-factly, 'They are receptacles.'"

"With these three words," Wilson continued, "her thoughts poured into my mind. In an instant she told me that what I was calling 'unacceptable' was all that these people's souls were capable of experiencing. I also felt her say something about their future; that their future and my future would be very different. I wasn't a part of them. I wasn't connected to 'humanity.'"

This has been a discussion of the good versus evil elements of abduction as perceived by many of the more widely known abductees and researchers. Obviously, there has been a wide range of opinions expressed here, and certainly the field is open to as many different beliefs as there are people having the experience.

In various instances, UFOs have actually taken the form of "signs and wonders" described in the Bible. Here a UFO photographed by police offiers is in the shape of a cross. Similar phenomena has been seen in recent years over various Middle East nations, particularly in time of war.

RETURN OF THE SON OF MAN IN THE CLOUDS
By Professor G.C. Schellhorn

The number of references in the Old and New Testament to clouds and the return of the Son of Man is surprising, even startling. Once we have become aware of the close relationship between clouds and spacecraft found in the scriptures, and add to that realization the fact that the Son of Man is prophesied to return "on the clouds,' the implication becomes stunning, to say the least.

These references begin in the Old Testament. For instance, in the Book of Daniel:

> *I saw in the night visions, and behold, with the clouds of heaven there came one like a son of man, and he came to the Ancient of Days and was presented before him. And to him was given dominion and glory and kingdom, that all peoples, nations, and languages should serve him; his dominion is an everlasting dominion, which shall not pass away, and his kingdom one that shall not be destroyed.*

Dan 7:13-14

We are told not only that "with the clouds of heaven there came one like a son of man" but that this son of man "was given dominion and glory and kingdom...." This dominion "is an everlasting dominion" and it "shall not pass away" and "not be destroyed." Here we have, as Bible scholars well know, an obvious reference to the messiah, either to Jesus, if one is a Christian, or to a messiah yet to appear for the first time, if one is Hebrew. If one is Buddhist, Hindu or Hopi, it is also a repeat of an earlier phenomenon. Some Moslems likewise look forward to the appearance of a special Mahdi to set aright a confused and increasingly godless world.

That this messiah will not (again) come tenderly is made quite clear in Isaiah:

> *'For behold, the Lord will come in fire, and his chariots like the stormwind, to render his anger in fury, and his rebuke with flames of fire. For by fire will the Lord execute judgment, and by his sword, upon all flesh; and those slain by the Lord shall be many.'*

Is 66:15-16

FLYING SAUCERS IN THE HOLY BIBLE

Are these 'chariots like the stormwind' unfamiliar? We have already seen so many examples of them associated, as here, with 'fire.' The remaking of the earth this time is not by water but fire. Aren't we quite logical, then, under the circumstances, in wondering if this fire might not be atomic fire unleashed by our own hand and precipitating a nuclear holocaust?

In Matthew we are told how Jesus leads Peter, John and James, his brother, up a high mountain:

> *And he was transfigured before them, and his face shone like the sun, and his garments became white as light. And behold, there appeared to them Moses and Elijah, talking with him. And Peter said to Jesus, 'Lord, it is well that we are here; if you wish, I will make three booths here, one for you and one for Moses and one for Elijah.' He was still speaking, when lo, g bright cloud overshadowed them, and a voice from the cloud said, 'This is my beloved Son, with whom I am well pleased; listen to him.' When the disciples heard this, they fell on their faces, and were filled with awe. But Jesus came and touched them, saying, 'Rise, and have no fear.' And when they lifted up their eyes, they saw no one but Jesus only.*

Mt. 17:2-8

Several things about this passage should give us pause for thought. No wonder the disciples are filled with "awe." What they are seeing is extraordinary. The "bright cloud," it makes sense to assume, is reference to a hovering spacecraft. The commander of the craft communicates with ground level by means of a loudspeaker. Undoubtedly those at ground level who had never seen a spacecraft reflecting the sun and heard a voice emanating from it would be very impressed, even overwhelmed. The disciples surely are. They "fell on their faces." Not only is the man they follow extraordinary, but he leads them literally and figuratively to extraordinary, out-of-this world experiences.

Now, we have got to ask, just *where in the world* did Moses and Elijah come from? This is the same Moses who talked directly with "God" well over a thousand years before Jesus was born. This is the very same Elijah who also talked with "God" and who was translated (transported) at last out of this world, perhaps aboard a spacecraft, just as Enoch had been. The easy answer is to say, God can do anything. The skeptic might say the disciples are experiencing an optical illusion or a mass hallucination--that the bright sun got to them this particular day.

FLYING SAUCERS IN THE HOLY BIBLE

I don't pretend to know for sure all the answers to the questions this puzzling scene raises. But I have some ideas. They have to do with the dilation of time effect at high speeds, which is an accepted fact among our scientists today. We need to understand that as speeds approach closer to the speed of light, such as in a fast moving (or orbiting) spacecraft, the passage of time, as we know it on earth, slows. A living physical body traveling at, say, 100,000 miles per second in a spacecraft ages less fast, much slower than the same body or a like body left on planet earth. All of this can be calculated mathematically, of course, according to formulae. Time is a variable product, it would seem, depending upon the mix of energy, speed and distance. So what are we really saying, then?

The time dilation effect can lead to some startling results. Our children may fly off some day to visit stars and planets many light-years from earth. When they return, only a few years or decades older, earth will have aged tens of thousands of years. It would indeed be a different world, unrecognizable perhaps, with no chance of seeing past acquaintances and loved ones. In a way, Thomas Wolfe, the novelist, was far more accurate than he himself knew for our space travelers when he titled one work, *You Can't Go Home Again*.

What does all this have to do with Peter's and James' and John's experience? Simply this. It is scientifically possible that they were actually looking at the original Moses and Elijah. If Moses and Elijah were transported in body aboard a spacecraft more than a millennium before, and that craft had been flying at speeds close to the speed of light, or even beyond it, they would only be a few years older at the most than they had been when first taken aboard ship. *And Jesus Christ, if he returned today or in the near future as commander of a space fleet come to usher in a New Age and sweep out the old, could have, if he chose to, the same body he had two thousand years ago and it would have aged only slightly.*

The same could be said of Viracocha, an ancient astronaut who visited the Incas, or Buetzalcoatl, probably another extraterrestrial visitor, who influenced the Mayas and Aztecs greatly before taking his leave. The same principle would apply to any space visitor from our ancient past. Theoretically, any one of them could return to us today only slightly older and, one assumes, as fit and in as fine fettle as of yore.

The scene on the mountain suggests even more. Moses and Elijah and Jesus are working together, as if there is a plan, as if details and strategies are being worked out. And things are being done in the sight of these three disciples, who will record the vision and spread it over the world with the passage of time. Even to us, today. Once again we have evidence that extraterrestrial activity is the guiding hand for much of what transpires on earth, certainly for much of what happened in biblical times.

The idea of Jesus as an ancient astronaut, an enlightened entity from here or elsewhere who embodied as a human to live as an example to men and to teach and preach the potentiality within man, the kingdom to come that is realizable and which is the destiny of man if he wishes to be – that idea is supported by more evidence than many people, including theologians and governments, would like to believe. Didn't the Master say after all, 'You are from below, I am from above; you are of this world, I am not of this world'? (Jn 8:23)

That 'coming with the clouds of heaven,' as Mark quotes the Master as saying, (Mk 14:62) threatens too many vested interests, just as it called into question the life style of the masses and the theological and governmental practices of the era in which he walked the earth. He was preaching the kingdom to come, the style of life of a future New Age. He was not preaching himself, making himself into a cultish ritual as churches are wont to do with him today. The focus has been shifted and dangerously so. The governments of men, no matter how pathetic they may be, do not wish to relinquish their power over the destiny of men's lives. The churches, long corrupted, preach guilt and fear mixed with ritual, not real new life through the perfection of the mind and spirit of man under the tutelage of wiser, cosmic intelligence. The vision that present day popular government and popular religion hold out for man, amidst their squabbling, is a rather nebulous materialistic present, supported by false advertising and an inferior product, wedded to a future lacking spiritual growth and personal responsibility. The Master knew what man's true potential was and came to remind him in spite of what false priests and false governments might tell him:

> *'Truly, truly, I say to you, he who believes in me will also do the works that I do; and greater works than these will he do, because I go to the Father.*

Jn 14:12

It would appear that man's true potential is to develop mind and spirit to the degree that he can 'do the works that I do; and greater works than these....' There is no magic here. Cosmic laws are inviolable. Miracles happen when someone does something, using his greater knowledge of cosmic law, and it astounds the less knowledgeable in his presence. When man has reached the spiritual growth level that makes him capable and worthy of such knowledge, he will be the total master of the material world, capable of doing things that he thought formerly impossible or the doings of gods only:

> *'For truly, I say to you, if you have faith as a grain of mustard seed, you will say to this mountain, "Move hence to yonder place," and it will move; and nothing will be impossible to you.'*

Mt 17:20-21

FLYING SAUCERS IN THE HOLY BIBLE

Yes, even move mountains.'Nothing will be impossible to you.' That is the promise. In fact, the Master Jesus of Nazareth made additional reference to the potentiality of developing man when he said:

> *'Is it not written in your law, "I said, you are gods"'?*

Jn 10:34

He is quoting the 82nd Psalm ascribed to the seer Asaph, companion to David:

> *They have neither knowledge nor understanding, they walk about in darkness; all the foundations of the earth are shaken. I say, 'You are gods, sons of the Most High, all of you; nevertheless, you shall die like men, and fall like any prince.'*

Ps 82:5-7

The great message to men, who have been developed and guided by enlightened extraterrestrials whose mission was to help a fledgling species rise out of savagery -- that great message is the destiny of their own godliness, equaling the spiritual and mental development even of those who nurtured them. It is a destiny with potential seemingly without limit. One recalls again the words of the "Lord" in Genesis:

> *And the Lord said,'Behold, they are one people, and they have all one language; and this is only the beginning of what they will do; and nothing that they propose to do will now be impossible for them'*

Gen 11:6

But there are certain conditions. There is danger along the way. The psalmist says,'nevertheless, you shall die like men, and fall like any prince.' Like any mortal prince. It appears that man is seen by the psalmist as yet an imperfect creation, a transitional being, and at his present state of development, he is heir to his human mortality. He is not guaranteed everlasting life as are the true Sons of God. The Master in his references to the 82nd Psalm does not contradict him. But he offers the vision, the future. The danger is ego and selfishness.

The "serpent" in the Garden of Eden knew the potential of man:

92

FLYING SAUCERS IN THE HOLY BIBLE

But the serpent said to the woman,'You will not die. For God knows that when you eat of it your eyes will be opened, and you will be like God, knowing good and evil.'

Gen 3:4-5

Ah! to 'be like God'! To know so much! The danger to man is doublepronged. He can be slothful and lazy, a Russian Oblomov who sleeps his life away and his opportunities for mental and spiritual growth. Or, like Goethe's Dr. Faust, he can insist on learning things which are counterproductive or which he is not mentally and spiritually developed enough to cope with successfully. Thus we have the extraterrestrial commander in Genesis putting a break to man's premature attempt to reach the heavens:

And the Lord said,'Behold, they are one people, and they have all one language; and this is only the beginning of what they will do; and nothing that they propose to do will now be impossible for them. Come, let us go down, and there confuse their language, that they may not understand one another's speech.' So the Lord scattered them abroad from there over the face of all the earth, and they left off building the city.

Gen 11:6-8

But man insists on reaching for the heavens. He will not long be put off. There is something innate in him that makes him reach out and upward to understand the world, the universe and its Creative Force, to imitate creation and emulate₁ his God. Perhaps no one has written better of this relentless urge of man's spirit to strive upwards than the fourteenth century German mystic, Meister Eckhart:

Even so the mind, unsatisfied with infernal light, will press through the firmament and press through the heavens to find the breath that spins them. Yet this does not satisfy it. It must press farther into the vortex, into the primal region where the breath has its source. Such a mind knows no time nor number: number does not exist apart from the malady of time. Other root, the mind has none save in eternity. It must surpass all number and break through multiplicity. Then it will be itself broken through by God, but just as God breaks through me, so I again break through Him. God leads this spirit into the wilderness and into the oneness of its own self.... (Translated by C.de B. Evans)

93

FLYING SAUCERS IN THE HOLY BIBLE

The New Testament is filled with references to the enlightened messiah coming 'on the clouds' to set man's striving, which has lost its direction, back on course:

> *'Immediately after the tribulation of those days the sun will be darkened, and the moon will not give its light, and the stars will fall from heaven, and the powers of the heavens will be shaken; then will appear the sign of the Son of man in heaven, and then all the tribes of the earth will mourn, and they will see the Son of man coming on the clouds of heaven with power and great glory; and he will send out his angels with a loud trumpet call, and they will gather his elect from the four winds, from one end of heaven to the other.'*

Mt 24:2931

In the Gospel of Matthew, after a description of great earth changes, perhaps even an axis shift, the messiah is seen 'coming on the clouds of heaven with power....' Is it presumptuous to suggest that the gathering of 'his elect from the four winds' has not already begun? The increased UFO activity of the last few years which is worldwide in scope makes this idea distinctly possible, if not probable.

The Gospel of Luke also speaks of the messiah coming out of the clouds:

> *'And there will be signs in sun and moon and stars, and upon the earth distress of nations in perplexity at the roaring of the sea and the waves, men fainting with fear and with foreboding of what is coming on the world; for the powers of the heavens will be shaken. And then they will see the Son of man coming in a cloud with power and great glory. Now when these things begin to take place, look up and raise your heads, because your redemption is drawing near.'*

Lk 21:2528

First we have another indication of great earth changes preceding the event. Then the Son of Man comes 'in a cloud.' Must we be so literal as to suppose, as so many theologians do, that this particular day is simply overcast or that the clouds somehow represent a metaphor for 'great glory'3 It seems as likely or more likely that the 'cloud' is biblical language for either extraterrestrial craft or the cloud cover they manufacture or use to veil themselves, evidence of which is plentiful from both past and present.

FLYING SAUCERS IN THE HOLY BIBLE

When Paul writes in 1 Thessalonians, he uses similar language to Matthew and Luke:

> *...then we who are alive, who are left, shall be caught up together*
> *with them in the clouds to meet the Lord in the air; and so we shall*
> *always be with the Lord.*

1 Th 4:17

The traditional explanation for these statements is vague and unsatisfying, usually a sketchy idea of some kind of divine supernatural levitation about which we aren't suppose to ask too many embarrassing questions. However, the ability of present-day extraterrestrial craft to transport or levitate physical bodies, including cows, cars and men, from ground level into a hovering craft has been witnessed or experienced by more than one person. (See Andrews' *Extraterrestrials Among Us* and Hopkins' *Intruders*.) It makes sense to view this kind of scene in a new light. Then we can visualize the apotheosized Adam, Jesus Christ, arriving with his extraterrestrial friends to aid the elect and the "first fruits" in the extremity of the moment. These individuals are to be saved not only because of their spiritual attainment but also possibly to help re-establish, and repopulate, a better new earth. They are "caught up together...in the clouds to meet the Lord in the air...." The "Lord in the air" is the messiah, the Christ. And he is aboard a spacecraft, with other spacecraft hovering near to carry out *the plan*, to bring to fruition the Great Experiment.

Finally, we need to take a look at Revelation and what it tells us about the messiah coming out of the clouds. It will serve as a kind of capstone to our discussion of Jesus Christ, messiah and astronaut.

St. John gives us the most dramatic pictures of the returning messiah. Early on in Revelation, we get our first glimpse:

> *Behold, he is coming with the clouds, and every eye will see him,*
> *every one who pierced him; and ail tribes of the earth will wail on*
> *account of him. Even so. Amen.*

Rev 1:7

The "clouds" will be with him. Here again we have the use of a plural. There is more than one craft. There is a fleet. "Every eye will see him." Already, a large number of human beings have seen UFOs with their own eyes. The Gallup polls taken in the past are quite revealing about the public attitude toward the "phenomenon." The 1966 poll indicated that

40% of the population believed that UFOs are real. By 1984 the figure had jumped to 80%. We might suppose that with the increased exposure the population has had to UFOs – and a planned one, it would seem, like a gradual acclimating – that the appearance of a fleet of spacecraft during the calamitous happenings of an "end time" situation would be not only awe inspiring but also something that the eyes and minds of the masses would recognize as being biblically related and then draw the appropriate conclusions.

> *Then I looked, and lo, a white cloud, and seated on the cloud one like a son of man, with a golden crown on his head, and a sharp sickle in his hand.*

Rev 14:14

The description gets more specific now. The "cloud" is a "white cloud" and one "like a son of man," an extraterrestrial follower of the messiah, is actually "seated on the cloud...." Seated in the "cloud," in the craft would be a more accurate translation but the meaning seems clear enough, unless someone wishes to maintain that the "man" is sitting on fleecy billows of wispy air just before he helps clean up mother earth's house.

Revelation continues with its own description of "end time" and the earth changes accompanying the moment. Then in chapter nineteen we are given a final striking account of the descent of the messiah himself to earth:

> *And the angel said to me,'Write this: Blessed are those who are invited to the marriage supper of the Lamb.' And he said to me,'These are true words of God.' Then I fell down at his feet to worship him, but he said to me,'You must not do that! I am a fellow servant with you and your brethren who hold the testimony of Jesus. Worship God.' For the testimony of Jesus is the spirit of prophecy. Then I saw heaven opened, and behold, a white horse! He who sat upon it is called Faithful and True, and in righteousness he judges and makes war.*

Rev 19:9-11

Notice that the angel-crewman accompanying the messiah cautions John not to worship the crew members themselves, which man was so accustomed to doing in biblical times, making gods out of extraterrestrial craft commanders and crewmen alike. He is only a 'fellow servant,' like John and his brethren.'Worship God,' he advises. This "God" of which the "angel" speaks is not an extraterrestrial spaceship commander, I take it, but the real thing, the Greater God of both earthlings and extraterrestrials alike. And one of his servants is the man who overcame the most adversity on earth, perfected himself so well that he achieved a greater oneness with this Greater God in his earth life (lives) and perhaps existences elsewhere than any entity who has walked the paths of this world – this Jesus the Master who became the Christ.

"Behold, a white horse!" The "heaven opened" and he who is called "Faithful and True," the messiah, descends. The "white horse" analogy, which I take to be another attempt to describe and make acceptable the spacecraft idea to an earlier mankind, is repeated in Indian scriptures (in Krishna's, the Kalki avatar's, return), the Maitreya Buddha's appearance, the Mazdean savior Sosiosh's appearance and others. Could it be that it is not accidental that these various religions have so much in common in the descriptions of the return of their avatars, of the appearance of their messiahs? The temptation is to say that the cultural impetus to believe in such returns is not accidental but has a distant though similar factual base from which to build – the existence of extraterrestrial visitors who paved the way for their return.

Excerpted From The Book
ETS IN BIBLICAL PROPHECY
by Professor G. C. Schellhorn
Used by Permission of the
Publisher - Horus House Press

The Assumption of the Virgin
By ANON Painted c.1490

UFOS IN THE PRESENT DAY HOLY LAND

By Sean Casteel

While most of this book is focused on UFOs and their frequent appearances in the pages of the Bible, there is a wealth of interesting sightings and abduction cases from present day Israel that are also worthy of mention here.

Perhaps the best-known Israeli UFO researcher is journalist and author Barry Chamish. In this chapter we will look at some of the more exciting case histories Chamish has collected over the years, and then move on to look at the prophetic aspects of the sightings witnessed in Israel since the late Nineteenth Century.

THE UFOs FIND BARRY CHAMISH

It is quite common for someone with little or no interest to stumble onto the UFO phenomenon through no conscious intent of their own. Such is the case with Barry Chamish, who was serving in the Israeli Air Force in the early 1980s when he and a comrade-in-arms, Adam Reuter, sighted strange objects flying over their post in the desert. The strange sightings continued for more than three months, and, over time, were seen by nearly everyone at the airbase.

The objects bore no resemblance to what they had been trained to identify as part of their military education, and when Chamish reported the UFOs to his superior officers, he was told to ask no further questions and to tell no one else what he and his friend had witnessed. As word spread through the other airmen at the installation, Chamish was singled out for the usual ridicule that typically accompanies a person's decision to honestly report what they have seen.

"As the summer wore on," Chamish writes, "Adam and I were the sole advocates of the UFO theory, and I especially was subjected to mockery. The most common theory among the unit was that a new weapons system was being tested, but over time, that explanation did not suit even the most hardened critics.

"One morning at assembly," Chamish continued, "the unit asked our officers to request an explanation from the Air Force. A few days after the request was submitted, a colonel from the Meteorological Division came down and addressed us. His message was plain and simple, 'We don't know what you are seeing but we request that you do not talk about your sightings and do not tell outsiders since that only spreads rumors.' So the arguments over the lights continued, and as the strongest advocate of the extraterrestrial visitation hypothesis, I was ribbed ruthlessly."

At that point, Chamish adds a dramatic statement to the mix.

FLYING SAUCERS IN THE HOLY BIBLE

"This would not happen today. Back in 1980, very few Israelis had seen UFOs."

The implication being, of course, that sightings in Israel became so commonplace that there are few doubters left there anymore.

CONFIRMATION OF THE UNKNOWN

In spite of all the ridicule he endured, Chamish was intrigued enough to begin some investigating of his own. He quizzed some of the pilots at his airbase about whether they had ever encountered UFOs themselves.

"I was serving at a large Air Force Base, and pilots would occasionally lecture us on tactics for aiming and shooting our missiles. Once the lecture ended, I approached the pilots and asked them if they had ever chased UFOs.

"Because I was a fellow soldier, the pilots let down their guard. Two admitted that they had chased ships of unexplainable origin. One was glowing blue and the pilot chased it over Haifa until it tired of the pursuit and sped over the Mediterranean at a speed the pilot's state-of-the-art Phantom could never hope to achieve. The other chase was over Jerusalem. The object was red in color, twice as large as a Phantom and 'disappeared before my eyes.'"

Chamish was later told that he had had a rare privilege in getting a pilot to talk to him at all. A reporter for the official magazine of the Israeli Air Force, identified only as "Julie," was doing a story about the UFO wave and was interviewing some of the same people as Chamish was for his own research.

"She told me outright,ö Chamish said, ôthat there is a special unit within the Air Force investigating UFO incidents but as far as anyone was concerned, it was non-existent. The Air Force would not help one of its own journalists get near the unit or its files. And pilots were ordered not to answer her questions."

Chamish told the story of a former Air Force radar operator who spoke to him.

"He told me, 'The operators often get strange blips on their screens, such as objects flying at impossible speeds which shouldn't be there or objects making gravity-defying turns. These are reported and planes scrambled to chase them. I was personally responsible for two reports that led to chases. I saw the pictures the pilots took. They were of cigar-shaped craft. The Air Force feels these craft are intruders and a security risk so it will not publicize such incidents, partly to avoid panic and in part because there is no answer to them if they turn hostile.'

"Because the Air Force had effectively covered up UFO encounters," Chamish continued, "and because there were so few sightings, until the late 1980s almost all Israelis viewed UFOs as pure science fiction. Then, in 1988, two UFO incidents were well filmed and documentary evidence was presented to the public."

FLYING SAUCERS IN THE HOLY BIBLE

THE MODERN ISRAELI UFO FLAP BEGINS

Chamish recounts the amazing story of the initial salvoes in the modern Israeli UFO wave.

"On the 26th of February, 1988, Rosetta Kalphon was having a gathering at her apartment in Haifa on Israel's northern Mediterranean coast. Included among her fifteen guests was a professional photographer from Ashdod who had brought his video camera with him. As the evening drew to a close, all sixteen people stood on Rosetta's balcony and watched a spectacular UFO, while for seventeen minutes it was filmed professionally. Shortly after, journalists were invited to Rosetta's apartment to view the film."

Chamish was not present with those first journalists, but he did see a frame of the film reproduced in a local newspaper.

"The UFO is somewhat umbrella-shaped," he said, "and on the side shown in the shot were eight smallish orange lights and, in the middle of them, an orange light twice their size."

Later, on June 26 of that same year, the Israeli papers carried an account by one Yossi Ayalon.

"Two nights before," Chamish writes, "at 1:30 AM, he stood on his balcony in Herzlia, ten miles north of Tel Aviv, and saw a point of light appear on the horizon out of nowhere. 'I called my wife,' Ayalon reported to the newspaper, 'but the light had disappeared by then. Suddenly it reappeared as big and bright as the sun at dawn. I knew I was seeing something strange – something I'd never witnessed before, so I ran inside for my video camera and started filming.'"

Chamish takes up the story again.

"Yossi did not call the police," he said, "but rather sent the film to Israel Television for public scrutiny. He, however, refused to appear on television, explaining, 'I never believed in UFO stories and I don't want to become a joke. But I just can't ignore what I filmed and what I saw.'

"Nor could many viewers. Yossi's UFO is clearly round and like many of the Israeli UFOs, emits a bright orange light. The roundness is broken by a dark colored square from the rim in the middle, taking up about twenty percent of the ship's size.

"Thus, in 1988, two UFOs were videotaped in Israel, and this evidence is important to me," Chamish solemnly states. "Only by gathering the strongest physical evidence in the present could the more difficult Biblical thesis be made possible."

In other words, if we choose to believe that UFOs interacted on numerous occasions with the personages of the Bible, it is essential to prove the reality of UFOs in the present day to make that belief in ancient encounters truly concrete.

FLYING SAUCERS IN THE HOLY BIBLE

MODERN ISRAELI ABDUCTEES

After the initial trickle of sightings reported above, a virtual flood of UFO reports began in Israel, many of which were documented by videotapes that fully supported the claims of witnesses. And just as it takes place throughout the world, the strange phenomenon quickly jumped from simple UFO sightings reports to the ever-increasingly complex abduction accounts.

In one of his numerous articles, Chamish relates the history of three Israeli abductees, the first of whom is Ada, a medical electronics technician from Kfar Saba.

Ada's testimony begins: "In the afternoon after work during the summer of 1993, I went to my bedroom to sleep. I saw within a three-dimensional being less than a meter from me. He was tall and wearing a 'spacesuit' of silver and green. The being emitted white beams from his waist area. I felt the energy of the beams first in my feet, then throughout my whole body. The feeling was wonderful. A feeling of fullness, well-being, joy and purity. Then the being left. It took small steps and it was gone. For weeks I walked around with this feeling of fullness. My views on life and death have changed since then. When I am not afraid, I can let loose and call up visions of all kinds of beings. I feel their presence everywhere, in my home, my car and other places.

"That year, despite my overall feelings of warmth, I was often very tired and slept too much. In this period, they helped me in many ways, even finding a complete solution to my problems with my husband. I couldn't complain about this first learning period."

The aliens at some point leave behind a calling card on Ada's body, a series of 20 blue spots, what she called "tiny blood dots."

"The spots went away in two days," she continues, "and then the aliens returned in the middle of the night. They literally smothered me with a feeling of love, and I felt a wave of heat. That night, a sinus abscess that I had suffered for ten years disappeared.

"I was told that there are two types of aliens, good and bad. The good wish to promote harmony, but the bad have the upper hand right now. They are responsible for the UFO landings and the mass abductions and have no concept of the pain they cause."

The next story Chamish offers is that of a woman named Chani Salomon.

"On May 2, 1997, during the afternoon rest time, I felt a presence in the bedroom. I tried getting out of the bed, but failed. I saw an elliptical image 60 centimeters high of a brightly lit and glowing object. It approached me and I felt it was operating on me. It was a most uncomfortable feeling. My eyes were wide open and I saw what was happening to me, but I was helpless to react. A most worrying situation. I felt I was being drilled into from place to place. The center of the operation was in the heart. I felt a pain there that is indescribable. I was that unfamiliar with it.

101

FLYING SAUCERS IN THE HOLY BIBLE

"I tried to scream to alert my family, but no sound came out. I tried to say Shma Yisrael [which Chamish explains is a holy Jewish prayer, traditionally recited before death] but don't recall how many times. I went to the beach a few days later and saw all the people glowing and translucent. Then I felt an odd sensation in my forehead, between my eyes. The rest of the week, the area behind my ears hurt, though there was no sign of injury or wound. Two weeks after the first incident, I had a dream connected to UFOs, something which never happened before. In it, I'm with a group of people and we're all startled by the appearance of UFOs in the sky. A voice asks for volunteers to go up in the craft. A white beam lights up my knees, though I don't recall volunteering. The dream awakened me to the fact that there are others in the cosmos trying to reach us and help us. We just have to be sensitive to the infinite pool of energy and exploit it for our own health and care."

The third case Chamish gives details of was first published in a Tel Aviv newspaper on May 30, 1997. Chamish said he was initially reluctant to include it because the experiencer was not named in the article, but decided to go ahead with it because of the newspaper's reputation for integrity.

"The witness describes herself as a rationalist and a skeptic, then tells her frightening story," Chamish says by way of introduction.

"Things began almost innocently," the anonymous woman said. "I would have the sensation at night of being between sleep and a dream state, something that was difficult to control. Every morning I'd wake up confused, with deep pains centered around my right ear. Then I'd go to sleep at night and have the feeling I was choking, like I was breathing in smoke.

"Strange beings would appear in the dreams. Sometimes they'd be tall and long haired, with a stunted nose and giant nostrils, and sometimes like bald, skinny children with a mask-like face and huge eyes. After the dreams, I felt pain in the legs and the armpits, which included sores that disappeared later. I would feel that time was lost and I was very tired. For six or seven days, we experienced electrical blackouts whose cause was not known.

"On May 14, 1997, at night, I awoke from my sleep. But I felt tied down to the bed. I felt like I was choking, and my throat burned like I had drunk something caustic. The house stank of a crippling odor. I went into panic. I felt a smothering, heavy feeling in the atmosphere. The smell even emanated from my son's room.

"I could sit up in bed, and did so. Half an hour later I heard a sound in my ears which began like a cricket chirping and ended like a jackhammer. The sound emanated from somewhere above me. When the sound dissipated, I went downstairs and saw a shocking image: the windows and blinds were covered with a fluorescent blue light whose source seemed to be in the room, flowing outside. In the morning, I saw two of my photos scratched and torn like rats bit it, a sculpture had its throat damaged, and a doll's face was ripped off.

FLYING SAUCERS IN THE HOLY BIBLE

"Outside were two twenty-centimeter black circles that stunk of last night's smell. Around the twenty-centimeter circles were a number of eight-centimeter circles that formed the shape of a scorpion's tail. I'm not a paranoiac, but I have a feeling I've been violated inside. I think they've formed a bond with me and will be back. Especially the little ones with the big eyes."

It should be obvious to the reader that the abduction experiences the three women reported are very similar to stories told in the United States and throughout the world. The aliens come by night, typically terrify the abductee, and often leave little medical anomalies behind them in their wake. The feeling of being loved by the aliens, or of forming a "bond" with them as reported in the third case above, are also quite commonly reported by abductees worldwide.

THE "DEMONS"

Among the many strange case histories collected by Chamish are some extremely eerie instances of Arab Israelis encountering what they the believe are demons. Chamish sites some cases reported in the respectable daily newspapers *Yediot Ahronot* and *Maariv*.

"Dr. Harav Ibn Bari, a physician at Hasharon Hospital in Petach Tikveh, was returning from Beersheva by car with his cousin Dudi Muhmad at the wheel. He relates, 'After passing the bridge to Tel Aviv at 3:30 AM, I saw a strange figure on the opposite side of the road. We did a U-turn and stopped the car. The figure came out of the shadows and into the light. He was small, and his body color light. He lifted his right leg and approached us at terrific speed. He had huge, bulging, round black eyes. They contrasted with the white color around them. It was as if he was reading my thoughts and I couldn't take my eyes off his for six seconds. He lifted his right hand and Muhmad pressed on the gas and took off.'"

A few days later, Chamish writes, another similarly frightening episode occurred. "Khaj Muhmad Jamal Kavah, 45, a Tel Aviv cab driver who lives in the Arab village of Al-Arian, met his cousin Ataf Kavah at 6 PM at Mei-Ami Junction to drive to a dinner party. 'I saw him and signaled that he wait a moment while I relieved myself first. I head him say, 'Okay.' When I was finished I approached the car and saw that Ataf was wearing a shiny suit. I thought to myself, in his whole life, Ataf never wore material like that. I bent down to open the door and saw that Ataf wasn't sitting in the driver's seat. I stared over but the driver paid no attention to me. Then I saw the weird creature. He had long hair reaching to his shoulders, his nose was enormous like an eggplant, colored purplish black. I almost had a heart attack. But I regained my senses and began walking backwards towards the highway. My plan was to make a break for the cars if he followed me. But I couldn't run because I felt something holding me in place for fifteen minutes. Then Ataf opened the door and came out

103

looking totally confused. I shouted at him, 'You're not Ataf. What do you want from me?' Ataf recalls sitting in the car and wondering why it was taking Muhmad so long to get in. He got out of the car and asked him what he was waiting for. He remembers Muhmad yelling, 'You're not Ataf. Who are you? Where's the shiny suit you were wearing?'"

Chamish goes on to say that Muhmad took and passed a polygraph test arranged for him by one of the newspapers. Muhmad's home "became a pilgrimage center as dozens of people a day came to hear his story. Included among them are Muslim religious leaders who have concluded that Muhmad met a demon and irritated him by relieving himself in his territory. They say the demons are rising because so many Arabs are straying from their religion."

STILL MORE STRANGE ENCOUNTERS

A few more days passed and still another incident occurred. This time the victim was named Eli Hawald, a 33-year-old resident of a village near Haifa called Kfar Hawald.

"The tiny village has no electricity," Chamish begins, "and when Eli Hawald went outside at 11:00 PM, all was too clear for him."

"Out of nowhere, I saw a gigantic green light, "Hawald said, "the color of a traffic light, fall out of the sky. I ran into the house, locked the door, and watched from the window. When the craft was about ten meters above the ground, the light was dimmed and three figures were 'shot' to the ground from it. I began to shake.

"They had humanlike bodies," Hawalt continued, "but because they were 20 meters from my house, I couldn't distinguish their faces, just their color, which was completely black. They acted oddly. They would fan out, quickly return to one formation, and fan out again. I remember two things distinctly. They reformed after a siren was sounded that resembled puppies crying. And their speed was fantastic, tens of meters in two seconds. At this point, I alerted my wife and children and we escaped through the back door."

And the spate of demon encounters continued. Again, Chamish's source was the respected newspaper *Yediot Ahronot*.

"A Jenin resident picked up a hitchhiker on the Jenin-Dotan road. A few moments after he sat in the front seat, the driver looked at him and saw his face had become that of a dog with one eye. The driver stopped his car, got out and fainted after he saw the hitchhiker disappear. That incident has become the talk of Jenin. Some of the religious leaders believe that the passenger was a demon who lives in the area. Others believe he is a devil known as The Blind Liar who has returned to presage the arrival of the messiah. The driver is still in shock and is being treated at the Jenin Hospital."

The use of the guise of a dog in that last story is very interesting. Traditionally, dogs are regarded as "unclean" animals by Jews and Moslems both, and the idea that an "unclean" spirit or demon would make some kind of use of that tradition symbolically is not much of a stretch.

Chamish concludes by saying, "I make no claims to understanding why there has been a wave of demon-like entities witnessed among Israeli Arabs in the past year. But I can verify that the wave has been characterized by the high quality of the testimony associated with it. If one can generalize, Israeli Jewish encounters since 1993 have mostly been with giant entities and UFO activity has always accompanied the incidents, while Arabs of the region are mostly encountering grotesque monsters, with less direct UFO activity involved. Both the giants and the monsters are capable of disappearing into thin air." (See the book: *Invisibility and Levitation* by Commander X for additional accounts of UFOs and invisibility.)

CHAMISH ABANDONS UFO RESEARCH

Unfortunately, Chamish eventually felt it prudent to leave his UFO research behind. That decision resulted from what he took to be direct harassment from the Israeli government and media, both of whom began to use his history of interest in the UFO phenomenon as a weapon to wage war against a controversial book Chamish had published about the cover-up involved in the assassination of Israeli Prime Minister Yitzhak Rabin.

"Yitzhak Rabin was not murdered by the patsy imprisoned for the crime," Chamish declared, "but rather by his own bodyguard in a coup from within his own political circles. I collected my findings into a book called *Who Murdered Yitzhak Rabin*, which was published in five languages. For exposing the truth about Rabin, I have gained a large number of enemies, no small number from within the Israeli ruling establishment. Their main proof that my Rabin research is wrong is because I wrote about UFOs, therefore, I must be a nut. My UFO work was badly affecting my credibility. So I chose to distance myself from it."

Chamish's decision leaves us all a little disappointed as well, but perhaps one day the situation will change and Ufology will become a respected science in its own right. If so, Chamish's diligent research into UFOs in Israel will be an important link in the chain of truth.

GARY STEARMAN AND THE CHARIOTS OF WONDER

Gary Stearman is a well-known author and co-host, with his partner Dr. J.R. Church, of a television program called "Prophecy In The News." Their ministry is based in Oklahoma City, and their weekly half hour program is broadcast on satellite and cable all over the world. They also publish a monthly magazine dealing with prophetic subjects. In an interview with Stearman conducted specifically for this book, the theological and prophetic aspects of the modern UFO phenomenon and its interaction with the modern state of Israel are given a thorough examination.

"The fact about UFOs," Stearman began, "is that they seem to correspond in many ways to what human beings have associated for centuries with spiritual events. There seems to be a spiritual quality within the UFO world and, specifically, it can be seen as part of perhaps a spiritual struggle.

"And with that in mind," he continued, "it's very useful to compare UFOs, the history of UFOs in the modern era, with the occurrences of UFOs in various parts of the world. First of all, the Bible speaks of fiery chariots. The chariot in Hebrew is called the *merkavah*. It has been suggested, in fact, several modern Israelis have suggested, that UFOs in the Hebrew be called *merkavah mophtim*. And *mophtim* means 'wonder.' So what you have in the Hebrew would be 'chariots of wonder,' or vehicles of wonder.

"And the vehicles of wonder have been seen in the Middle East literally for centuries. But in the modern era, particularly late 1947 through 1948 in Israel, they were seen not only in the United States and Europe, but also throughout the Middle East. They were reported as disc-shaped, sometimes cigar-shaped. Sometimes they were suspected of being Russian secret weapons. At other times, invasions from another planet. But they were nevertheless seen at the time."

THE TIMING OF THE UFO FLAPS

Stearman explained the pattern of how UFO sightings flaps were timed around crucial events in Israel.

"UFOs made their first dramatic appearance, really dramatic appearance, in 1947 and 1948. That would be the Jewish year 5708, or 47-48 in the Christian calendar. Of course, that was the year of the rebirth of Israel. And these were years when great battles were being fought by human beings in Israel, but the idea is that perhaps someone else was taking notice of this on a higher plane.

"Just about ten years later, in early October of 1956, during the great Sinai Campaign of Israel against Egypt, there were great numbers of sightings of UFOs. It was quite commonly reported in the newspapers of the Middle East, particularly the Israeli newspapers.

"And then again, in the Jewish year 5727, which of course was timed with late spring of 1967, the Six Day War erupted. When the Six Day War came to pass, there was a great UFO flap throughout the world. Then, during September and October of 1973, when the Yom Kippur War against Israel took place, sightings were again very common.

106

FLYING SAUCERS IN THE HOLY BIBLE

"So when you lay this out," Stearman said, "you have the years 1948, the date of Israel's statehood, and 1956, the Sinai Campaign, as well as 1961, when another massive anti-Israeli movement was begun, of Arabs against the Israelis, 1967, the Six Day War, and 1973, the Yom Kippur War. All of those were the dates of historic UFO flaps. So that's sort of the beginning thesis that leads us to other ideas."

ANOTHER RELEVANT SIGHTINGS WAVE

Stearman made another connection between a major UFO sightings wave and the modern state of Israel, with the surprising year being 1897.

"The beginning of the state of Israel," Stearman explained, "was in the year 1897. That was the great year of the first Zionist Congress in Basel, Switzerland. And in 1897, the world experienced, and I'm talking about the entire world-and it's heavily reported in all the UFO literature-the world experienced a flap of UFO sightings. But they were not called UFOs. They were called airships.

"I believe that the 1897 flap was timed with the rebirth of Israel. From 1897 to 1947 of course is precisely 50 years, and the two great UFO flaps happened in those years."

Stearman related a familiar anecdote from the 1897 flap.

"There was the famous case of Alexander Hamilton of Leroy, Kansas. April 21, 1897. An unidentified airship was sailing low over his farm and it lowered a rope and trapped one of his cattle. A two-year-old heifer, bawling and jumping, was lassoed and hauled up into this airship. And it flew away. Well, there is an affidavit published in a number of the UFO publications from Alexander Hamilton. It was signed by the local sheriff, the town banker, and the registrar of deeds, attesting that this really happened.

And there are just, as you know, dozens if not hundreds of reports from 1897. I link those to the first Zionist Congress, which essentially was the meeting that established the Zionist Movement and the state of Israel."

FROM ROSWELL TO THE PRESENT

"To me," Strearman said, "the biggest year in the history of Ufology is 1947, the year of the Roswell Incident, timed perfectly with the foundation of modern Israel. Of course, everyone's read about Roswell.

"I believe that the Roswell event actually had an effect on the shaping of the government of the United States, in that it established an Above Top Secret mentality in the old Army Air Corps, which later became the Air Force. And a brand new bureaucracy was established to keep secret the fact that we had been contacted by alien beings, and that they had crashed.

FLYING SAUCERS IN THE HOLY BIBLE

The most famous crash was at Roswell, New Mexico, but there are other reported crashes around that same time.

"And to bring this up to the present date," he continued, "right at the moment there is an incredible acceleration in UFO sightings, just in the last little while. Not just in Israel or the mideast, but over the entire planet. I think it coincides with Arial Sharon's declaration that the Temple Mount belongs to the Jewish people. He made that statement in September of the year 2001.

"And from that time to this, there have been just huge numbers of strange flying triangle sightings – low altitude flying triangles that move along very slowly are being seen all over the world now. I see that as a current wave of UFO activity, but again timed with extremely critical events in the Middle East. We're at a point where we may be at total war with Iraq, and of course Israel could become involved in that. If that happens, I would say that UFO reports will increase in an alarming manner."

BUT WHAT DOES IT ALL MEAN?

After Stearman had explained the timing of major UFO sightings waves with events in Israel, the question then became, "What does it all mean? What are the UFO occupants trying to say about their relationship to Israel?"

"Well," Stearman replied, "this takes us back to the fact that these are *merkavaim*, plural, and that's what the Bible calls them. The Bible speaks of the fiery chariots being like heavenly ambassadors, or sometimes they're called heavenly messengers, or angels. You can call them beings from another dimension. They're commonly called aliens. But the prophets of ancient Israel said that these were the watchmen watching over Israel. And they were acting on behalf of the people of Israel, according to the will of God. Now, that's what the Bible specifically says."

So did Stearman feel that the UFOs are making a show of force, letting the world know that they intend to protect Israel?

"Yeah, I do," he answered. "Or perhaps there is a battle, an ultra-dimensional battle, shall we say, a battle behind the scenes, taking place between those who favor one side or the other. You can state it any way you want to, but there's an earthly battle going on and there appears to be an ultra-dimensional battle going on, too."

Did Stearman mean something like the War In Heaven spoken of in the Bible's Book of Revelation?

"The War In Heaven, yeah," he said. "And it seems that every time Israel is threatened, the War In Heaven also seems to accelerate so that it becomes visible in this dimension as UFO and strange creature reports."

FLYING SAUCERS IN THE HOLY BIBLE

THE SERVANT'S EYES ARE OPENED

Stearman made reference to a story in the Bible, from Second Kings, Chapter Six, beginning in verse Fifteen.

"And when the servant of the man of God was risen early and gone forth," Stearman read aloud, "Behold, an host-that's an army-encompassed the city, both with horses and chariots. And his servant said unto him-of course 'he' being Elisha-the servant said unto him, 'Alas, my master, how shall we do?' In other words, we are in deep trouble. And he answered, 'Fear not, for they that be with us are more than they that be with them.' And Elisha prayed and said, 'Lord, I pray thee, open his eyes that he may see.' And the Lord opened the eyes of the young man who saw and behold the mount was full of horses and chariots of fire round about Elisha."

Stearman then illuminated the text a bit more.

"Now what was going on here in Second Kings, Chapter Six, is that there was a great battle being fought in which Israel was threatened, deeply threatened. And the prophet Elisha went out on behalf of Israel. The king of Syria had invaded Israel, and Elisha went down to deliver God's message to the leaders of Israel. And he had a servant with him. And the servant was deathly afraid that they were going to be killed, and Elisha prayed and the servant's eyes were opened and he was able to see that they were surrounded, the Israelites were surrounded by these chariots of fire, these *merkavim*. We could call them today the 'chariots of wonder.'

"And I believe this is an Old Testament reference to what we would call UFOs today, fighting on behalf of Israel."

SAME AS IT EVER WAS

"The same phenomenon exists today," Stearman concluded. "And so every time that Israel is threatened, the battle becomes pitched and becomes more visible to human eyes. And I believe that, Biblically speaking, you can make a strong defense for this because in the Old Testament, one of the titles of the Lord is 'Lord of Hosts,' or 'Jehovah of Hosts,' as he is called. And that title essentially is a military title. It's like being the General of the Heavenly Army.

"Of course, one of the major Bible themes is that the Lord fights on behalf of his people. In fact, one of the meanings of the name Israel is 'for whom God fights.' And so it can be very well said that the hosts of heaven are fighting on behalf of Israel and that each time Israel is in peril, what we call UFOs, but what really are probably better termed *merkeva mophtim*, these vehicles of wonder, these fiery chariots, roll into action on behalf of Israel."

109

UFO RELIGION – A NEW SPIRITUAL AWAKENING
By Tim Swartz

Brad Baker of Hartford City, Indiana was reluctant to talk about his UFO experience. Even though his encounter had occurred in 1985, Baker's fear of ridicule induced him to remain silent. That is, until a mutual friend, to whom he had confided his incredible tale, suggested that his story may be of interest to me. What Baker told me was not very different from the thousands of other "close-encounter" incidents that have been reported over the years. What made his story interesting was his opinion that the strange being he saw standing beside a landed disc-shaped object was none other than God himself.

"If it wasn't God, then it was Jesus," said Baker. "I know it sounds crazy, but the figure I saw looked just like those paintings you see of Jesus. He was wearing a long white robe and had long hair and a beard. He was standing in front of a bright-white light that looked to me to be somewhat shaped like a disc or an egg. What was really crazy is that when the light suddenly went out, there was nothing there. It was as if someone had turned off a television and the picture disappears."

Baker confessed that while he had never been a "church going kind of guy," after his incident he found himself interested in religion and spirituality.

"Seeing what I did convinced me that there is more going on then what we see in front of us," said Baker. "That figure looked so much like God that I am convinced that there is life on other planets and they could be messengers from God."

Incidents such as that experienced by Brad Baker are just the type of UFO-related reports that send most western UFO researchers heading for the door. The extraterrestrial hypothesis (ETH) has been singled out by many investigators as the most likely explanation for UFO sightings. However, what disturbs some researchers to the point that they exclude such reports, is the fact that a substantial number of UFO encounters involve what can be best described as spiritual or metaphysical experiences.

THE NATURE OF UFOs

Anyone who takes the time to diligently study the phenomena of UFOs, will eventually discover that there are no easy answers to be found. The research of UFOs has resisted all attempts to pigeonhole them into any one category. Since 1947 the belief has developed that UFOs are spacecraft operated by extraterrestrial visitors to our planet. This idea has become so predominate in our society that it is almost impossible to avoid the constant media influence that UFOs are being flown by extraterrestrial creatures.

Peter Davenport of the National UFO Reporting Center recently told MSNBC that reports

110

of UFOs probably involve spacecraft whose technology is beyond our current understanding. When asked his opinion of the nature of the visitors, and the purpose behind the visitations, Davenport replied:

"Those are the things that keep us motivated." However, he added. "I don't think there's any UFOlogist who has the answers to those questions. And if they do, you should probably reject their information."

After more than fifty years of investigation and research, no one has managed to offer a satisfactory explanation on the true nature of UFOs. However, UFOs and their associated phenomena continue to be reported. The skeptics have failed to convince those who have experienced UFOs that they were somehow mistaken. To these people, their experience was real and nothing can convince them otherwise.

Many UFO experiencers report that their encounter led to a complete change in their lives, often in a spiritual sense. Some have received additional visits by strange beings claiming to be highly advanced extraterrestrials who are here on Earth to save mankind from imminent danger. A few of these people have even been told that they were chosen by the Space People to act as a mouthpiece, or even a Messiah to lead the population to an eventual communion with the benevolent aliens.

Popular literature is full of such stories. These tales of gods and angels from outer space make most "nuts and bolts" UFO researchers uncomfortable, and sometimes even a little hostile. Some UFO investigators scorn the contactees who claim to have a psychic link with the Space Brothers. Walter Andrus of the Mutual UFO Network says such claims sound "a little bit like channeling, and we don't take much stock in channeling." Yet the recent history of UFOs seem to show that there have been deliberate attempts to connect the belief in otherworldly entities with spirituality and even religion. We could be now experiencing the birth of a new religion - a religion that combines scientific rationalism, spiritual beliefs and a hierarchy of semi-divine beings allegedly from other planets.

SCIENCE AS RELIGION

In ancient times God and his spiritual minions were everywhere. The daily rising and setting of the sun, in the thunderous lightning that split the sky in two, in the forests and glens that supplied an infant mankind with provisions and a sense of place in the world. Man walked the Earth and God existed in the heavens above. These were all the answers that were needed when the curious asked about the nature of the Universe and the secrets contained within.

Before long, these explanations were not enough and the inquisitive nature of man sought to unravel that which only God understood. Science was born and it quickly replaced God with the cold equations of mathematics. The old religions were dead, replaced by the new religion of Science.

However, science as a religion for the masses left a lot to be desired. Science preached an "It Just All Happened" philosophy that left no room for spiritual beings and a divine Creator. This belief system directly conflicted with the millenniums-old doctrines of a universe filled with Heavenly denizens. These deity-based beliefs were effective because they appealed to an instinct buried deep within all of us that seemed to acknowledge the basic reality of God.

Since the Nineteenth Century, science has enjoyed a tremendous following and has rewarded its believers with exciting discoveries and incredible technology. But, it is devoid of any spirituality or purpose. Organized religion resisted the temptations by branding new scientific discoveries as evil or heretical. Both faiths demanded total loyalty, there could be no middle ground, one or the other must be chosen.

To the average person this separation between science and spirituality made little sense. It seemed more realistic that the two were actually connected, eternally intertwined, one working with the other. A Creator made the Universe along with the laws of science to sustain it. It was obvious that reality was governed by scientific principles, but how did these principles arise in the first place? The Universe seemed a little too orderly to have all happened just by chance.

Unfortunately, religion and science remained unconvinced. Organized religion refused to change with time. It was becoming increasingly difficult to interest a modern audience in religious beliefs and dogmas that were developed by nomadic tribesmen thousands of years ago. And science was too busy enjoying its new found prestige to admit that there could be room for new and radical ideas. This conflict was the perfect catalyst for the creation of a new belief system. A system that took both science and religion to blend them into a new structure.

THE COMING OF THE GODS - AGAIN

People have asked why we don't see miracles today like those referred to in ancient religious writings. These old texts are filled with tales of angelic beings, strange wonders in the skies and divinely inspired prophets and their prophecies. However, these events are still occurring today on a daily basis throughout the world. Now, the wonders in the sky are silvery discs recorded on home video cameras. And rather then angels from God, we have spacemen from the Pleiades who are here to deliver prophetic messages of doom or salvation. The gods and goddesses of old have not gone away; they have merely traded in their long-white beards and togas for spacesuits and helmets.

FLYING SAUCERS IN THE HOLY BIBLE

When UFO contactees in the early 1950s began to tell of their alleged encounters with the pilots of UFOs, their stories seemed too fantastic for most to believe. Yet the tales of angelic Space Brothers – here to help guide mankind from its evil ways – struck a cord with those who were raised with scientific materialism.

Since science had supposedly proven that there was no place for God and angels in the universe, here instead were beings from another planet whose appearance and philosophies seemed more divine then physical. It was the perfect melding of spirituality and science. Superior beings from other worlds that were not only advanced technologically, but also spiritually.

The appearance of entities claiming to be from other worlds is not new to history. However, it was not until after 1947 that the belief in UFOs and extraterrestrials started to develop beyond a few individuals and science fiction novels. In a little more than fifty years we have seen a rapid evolution in the acceptance of alien creatures visiting our planet. This development is similar to past events that led to the creation of all major religions known today. It is therefore clear that we could be experiencing the genesis of a new spiritual system based on the belief of highly advanced, spiritual beings from outer space. The Space Age Religion.

HOW REAL ARE THE EXTRATERRESTRIALS?

In his book *Report on Communion*, author Ed Conroy writes: "...Students of the paranormal have often seen that UFO reports are known to have occurred during periods of other extremely unusual events that include poltergeist-like phenomena, reports of spontaneous human combustion, an upsurge in popular religious fervor and even - quite controversially – anomalous animal mutilations and disappearances."

It is true that many UFO cases involve reports that seem to be more ghostlike than real. UFOs and their occupants appear to be solid one minute and then vaporous the next. The alleged extraterrestrials have often seemed to be unduly concerned with the spiritual affairs of mankind. If anything, the UFOnauts act more like guardian angels than astronauts visiting for scientific explorations.

To those who have experienced the UFO phenomena, the event often begins by being struck by a blinding beam of light. John Keel writes in *The Eighth Tower*: "All great religions and countless cults began with the exposure of a single person to this phenomenon. Saul, Daniel, and other Biblical personages saw luminous phenomena at the outset of their adventures. They usually received messages and accurate prophecies. Later, when they passed the prophecies onto their friends and followers, those predictions usually came true. Because of this, they felt the holiness of their condition had been proven. The ranks of their followers grew. It was this process that inspired the spread of Christianity. In other ages the same process spawned the pagan religions and the myths of demonology."

Like the old religions, the Space Age religion has its hierarchy of divine and demonic beings. The angels are now played by the blond, nordic Space Brothers. While the devil and his demons are the big-eyed "Greys" that are believed responsible for an epidemic of UFO-related abductions that has dominated the UFO culture for over twenty years. It is amazing how quickly the mythology that now surrounds UFOs has grown and developed over the years. This is what will ground and sustain the Space Age religion over the rest of the millennium.

"This grounding and founding is maintained through the elaboration of particular ceremonies and rituals, especially the repetition of the content of the myth; the creation story. Each repetition of the foundational myth recreates those primary distinctions (such as 'flying saucer' or 'alien abduction') that bring a particular world into view; each successive re-creation holds the world in place," writes Keith Thompson, in his book *Aliens and Angels*. This is echoed by Holger Kalweit who states: "Perhaps the other world journey motif is 'camouflaged' in the modern lore of space travel which, like the fantastic voyage legends of the past, exemplifies what might be called the lure of the edge."

MISSIONARIES FROM THE STARS

Over the centuries, thousands of books have been written by people who claim to be channeling spirits, angels and even extraterrestrials. More than likely all of our great religious writings can be traced in part to messages received while in an altered state of consciousness. All of these trance-state communications read disturbingly the same, no matter if the source claims to be a divine being or alien entity from another galaxy. It has often been noted that channeled communications from supposed extraterrestrials sound so much like the messages received from angels and spirits that the two could be interchanged with little disruption.

Channeled communications from friendly extraterrestrials are given just about as much credence from researchers as tales of Santa Claus or the Easter Bunny. However, there are many reports of physical close encounters with UFO entities who seem interested in preaching their form of spirituality to witnesses, missionaries from the stars if you like.

On January 30, 1965, Sidney Padrick was taking a walk along Manresa Beach in California. Suddenly he heard a loud humming sound and saw a strange machine shaped like "two real thick saucers inverted." Padrick started to run away but was stopped by a voice that came from the object inviting him aboard. At the voices urging Padrick entered through a door that appeared in the side of the now landed saucer. Inside he was greeted by a medium-sized man with very pale skin, a sharp nose and chin and unusually long fingers. When Padrick asked for the man's name, he was told, "You may call me Zeeno."

Mr. Zeeno gave Padrick a quick tour of the craft which came with its own "chapel." Padrick remembered, "The color effect in that room was so pretty that I almost fainted when I went in. There were eight chairs, a stool, and what looked like an altar. Zeeno said: 'Would you like to pay your respects to the Supreme Deity?' I didn't know how to accept it, I'm forty-five years old, and until that night I had never felt the presence of the Supreme Being, but I did feel him that night."

In 1952, Cecil Michael of Bakersfield, California observed a flying saucer at close range, he subsequently had encounters with alleged aliens who took him away to their home planet. Michael claimed that the planet was orange in color, very hot and home to a strange creature that he called "the Devil."

"As I stood looking fearfully at the devil there was suddenly a bright white light that appeared besides me," recalled Michael. "In the middle of the light, Christ appeared in plain view . . . I turned to the Devil and, pointing my hand to the light, said, 'If you don't let me go, He will send for me.' The Devil responded: 'Yes, He is always interfering.'"

After spending almost three weeks on the alien planet, Michael was returned to Earth. Upon returning, the two extraterrestrials asked him to write the story of the incident with the Devil and Christ. "This is for the benefit of humanity," the aliens said. "We want the world to know about the great cosmic struggle between good and evil in which your planet is unknowingly involved."

Dr. Leopoldo Diaz of Guadalajara, Mexico says that in 1976 he had two contacts with beings who said they were from another planet. In the course of the visits the aliens told Dr. Diaz to proclaim the truth far and wide. His message was that "God is everywhere, all religions you profess on Earth are only roads to the same purpose - to know God."

These stories are just a few out of the hundreds of UFO close encounters that had religious undertones. The witnesses are often given the task by their contacts to deliver a message to the world, a message usually steeped in spiritual/religious connotations. Individually, none of these messages of salvation from the stars had much of an impact. But, collectively, over time, these stories serve to reinforce the UFO idea. The promise of hope from divine beings in the sky.

CARL JUNG ON UFOs

Shortly before his death, Carl Jung was one of the first to try and analyze UFOs in a symbolic way. In a 1951 letter to an American friend he wrote, "I'm puzzled to death about these phenomena, because I haven't been able yet to make out with sufficient certainty whether the whole thing is a rumor with concomitant singular and mass hallucination, or a downright fact."

In 1958, Jung concluded that it was more desirable for people to believe UFOs exist than to believe they don't exist. One of his final works, *Flying Saucers*, was an attempt to answer why it was more desirable to believe in their existence. Jung though that UFOs were examples of the phenomena of synchronicity where external events mirror internal psychic states. For Jung the UFO images had much to do with the ending of an era in history and the beginning of a new one. In his introductory remarks to *Flying Saucers* he wrote:

"As we know from ancient Egyptian history, they are manifestations of psychic changes which always appear at the end of one Platonic month and at the beginning of another. Apparently they are changes in the constellation of psychic dominants, of the archetypes, or 'Gods' as they used to be called, which bring about, or accompany, long-lasting transformations of the collective psyche. The transformation started in the historical era and left its traces first in the passing of the aeon of Taurus into that of Aries, and then of Aries into Pisces, whose beginning coincides with the rise of Christianity. We are now nearing that great change which may be expected when the spring point enters Aquarius."

In a manner similar to that which the medieval alchemists projected their psyche into matter, Jung felt that modern man projected his inner state into the heavens. In this sense, the UFOs became modern symbols for the ancient Gods which came to man's assistance in time of need.

Like the ancient visitations, the modern UFOs and aliens appear to be just as real and tangible, possessing intelligence and will that seem to go beyond mere projections of the inner psyche. A force that is independent of human existence, yet somehow influenced by it on an intimate level. In other words, if you believe in gods, demons, witches, fairies or flying saucer people, some intelligence, unknown by modern science, will adopt these roles and exist as long as there are believers. When the belief structure becomes outdated or forgotten, the entities will simply assume some other guise to continue their existence.

A DRIVING FORCE

This could be the driving force of religion and other spiritual beliefs since the beginning of time. In the past, some unknown intelligence wanted us all to believe in the gods. When monasticism became all the rage, the phenomena changed with the times and produced beings such as angels, the Virgin Mary and other holy entities. Now they have traded in their chariots for sleek futuristic flying saucers. However, there are still plenty of old religious beliefs around to keep visitations by figures like the Virgin Mary busy appearing to children and other believers.

116

FLYING SAUCERS IN THE HOLY BIBLE

The modern belief in extraterrestrial visitors springs not from the presentation of concrete evidence but from the repetition of the extraterrestrial "line" through thousands of contactees over the past fifty years or so. All of our religious beliefs have a similar basis, prophets who have allegedly talked with supernatural beings have spread the beliefs to the masses of people who have had no direct experiences with the phenomenon but are willing to accept the word of those who have.

It seems odd that aliens would be interested in our spiritual well-being. Richard Thompson writes in **Alien Identities** that extraterrestrials could be deliberately invoking mythological trappings to influence contacts. Thompson also theorizes that "UFO humanoids are not as alien to us as one might suppose. This is based on the argument that beings with humanlike form, humanlike emotions, and humanlike paranormal powers might be related to humans on a fundamental level."

The debate remains on just who or what is formulating this grand experience. From John Keel's mindless "Ultraterrestrials," Budd Hopkins big-eyed "Greys," Jacques Vallee's faceless "control group," Gordon Creighton's "Jinns," to Carl Jung's "projected collective psyche." All of these theories, on the surface, seem to offer viable explanations. Yet, none can totally claim to be the absolute truth. Perhaps portions from each can best explain the true nature of the phenomena. Some have argued that the spiritual aspects of certain UFO contacts are nothing more than an intellectually superior race using our superstitions to hide their true intent and purposes. Barbara Marciniak, who claims to be channeling messages from Pleiadians, reports that the creatures told her: "We refuse to be your answer. Just when you think you have us pinned down, we'll tell you something else. No one belief system can encompass all of reality in a complex universe."

John Keel has often stressed the significance of belief structures as related to UFO phenomena. "The phenomenon is dependent on belief," Keel writes in **The Mothman Prophecies**. "As more and more people believe in flying saucers from other planets, the lower force can manipulate more people through false illumination. I have been watching, with great consternation, the worldwide spread of the UFO belief and it's accompanying disease. If it continues unchecked we may face a time when universal acceptance of the fictitious space people will lead us to a modern faith in extraterrestrials that will enable them to interfere overtly in our affairs, just as the ancient gods ruled large segments of the population in the past."

While Keel may be overly alarmed about the process, his idea that there is a developing "faith" in extraterrestrials is almost certainly correct. Whether or not this faith is being postulated by true extraterrestrials, supernatural beings who mimic extraterrestrials, or our own unconscious minds, the fact remains that we are seeing an ancient process unfolding before us, with the creation of a new belief system, a new religion, as its ultimate goal.

117

FLYING SAUCERS IN THE HOLY BIBLE

THE WAR OF RELIGIONS

Since the early 1950's, a number of authors have postulated that UFOs may have connections to certain Christian beliefs and mythologies of the end times. The idea that UFOs and their occupants may actually be either angels or demons has captured the attention of many interested in religion and the UFO phenomena.

Either side of the debate can offer up substantial evidence to prove their point on the true nature of UFOs and their occupants. Christopher Montgomery in his manuscript *The Angel/UFO Hypothesis* states that: "Many ministers believe that aliens are not actually from another planet, but are demons disguising themselves as aliens in flying saucers. What a nefarious plot, I can think of nothing more sinister. That they are devils, and nothing good could come from a UFO. But what if I told you of an even more diabolical plot than that one. That would be that the fallen angels should try to convince us that they are from other planets, using UFO sightings to underscore their sincerity! This while knowing that the UFO is the only thing separating us from Satan's insatiable wrath. The Bible says that the fallen angel, Satan; '...walketh about, as a roaring lion, seeking whom he may devour.' Many people know that verse. But few are they that remember the rest of this famous passage. It says '...whom resist, steadfast in the faith!' We could take that one step further and say that UFOs are in fact angels, and further that this is just another example of the mysteries of the UFO and the Holy Bible paradigm."

Researcher John Thompson writes, "There is a definite God connection. As someone asked me, 'How do you know that 'they' don't come from an extraterrestrial dimension instead of a demonic one?' I told him, 'I don't.' But the truth is it does not really matter as nearly all alien reports fit with what religious writings have warned of for centuries. The aliens behind abductions are evil and the calling for help from God, if one believes in God, stops alien activity in the household or certainly brings it to a crawl.

"Now if they are extraterrestrial (ET) dimensional creatures from another Universe, so what? We still cannot physically touch them and they cannot touch us. Key abduction researchers with the aid of hypnosis, have said many abductees are breeding with aliens, hybrids, and even other humans. Many abductees have reported having 'perverted dreams,' It has to be concluded that these disturbing nightmares are the jelly that the best known researchers have made ET brick of.

"If there is sexual breeding between aliens and humans, and raping of humans by alleged hybrids – as some researchers claims – let us see proof. Such proof should constitute newly contacted unknown diseases and higher rates of sexually transmitted diseases in areas of high UFO sightings. If there is actual linkage between physical ET space craft and abductions that involve breeding games then the other linkage should also be there. Actually what they and others have done with their hypnosis sessions is a perversion to what is really going on. They have added great fog to the whole abduction issue. They have pulled out bits and pieces from abductees and constructed a partially completed puzzle that they would like to lay on a table.

"The problem is the 'bits and pieces' are only mental images and without independent witnesses and true physical proof there is no 'table' to lay them on. Despite doing two investigations myself from what I considered reliable witnesses who saw an alien associated with a physical airborne craft, in each instance the other witness accompanying them denied seeing the aliens. Indeed, in one case the other witness denied seeing any UFO or aliens at all!

"As these are the only two cases I've investigated that allegedly involved two witnesses seeing aliens near or inside perceived spacecraft, I have to conclude my initial witnesses were mistaken. It is only when we get into the realm of the true paranormal, and leaving UFOs out, that we get repeatable and multiple reports of what I call innerterrestrials (INT) sightings; the 'shadows' and 'haints' that have remarkable similarities to 'greys.' UFOs may actually be related to areas of high INT sightings and they may not. I have been told by a former pastor well-versed in the bible that the bible talks of 'manifestations.' Perhaps, more remarkable UFOs are only manifestations meant to deceive and confuse us. Since man can project holograms it is certainly conceivable that an unknown alien intelligence is manifesting craftier illusions.

"By-and-large, I'm concluded that after you factor out black budget UFOs, weather UFOs, piezoelectric UFOs – actually IFOs that most scientists or witnesses are not privy to or fully understand--heavenly bodies, common aircraft and bad witnesses, all we're left with is 'lights in the sky' and 'manifestations.' My point is, it has to be seriously entertained that there may be no true physical UFOs in our skies. Should there be no physical UFOs, although I remain open on this issue, then what remains are only INTs. The INTs, in turn, have helped abductees and hypnotherapists feed their own extraterrestrial UFO expectations. An idea that has been helped along by the mass media.

"Objectively, the facts don't support the UFO extraterrestrial hypothesis. This would explain why not a single person in the public domain has found one physical piece of evidence to support ET visitations. With millions now having seen UFOs over the last 50 years at least one tiny piece of a 'nuts and bolts' UFO should have been found by some lucky or determined individual in the general public. A few grams would be sufficient; yet, nothing. This total lack of physical proof also explains why many governments around the world have investigated UFOs, then abruptly halted their investigations. Objectivity has often killed many a splendid thought. The preponderance of evidence shows we are dealing with a nonphysical, dimensional intelligence that defies our concept of reality. We may wish it different but reality says otherwise."

FLYING SAUCERS IN THE HOLY BIBLE

The fact that many modern Biblical scholars' looks upon UFO phenomena with mistrust should come to no surprise – most religions exist in a state of perpetual hostility with each other – all believing that only their beliefs are the true path toward the Creator and salvation. It has been recognized by some experts that certain aspects in the belief of extraterrestrial UFOs have taken on a religious perspective. These emerging belief structures are seen as a threat to the current religious hierarchies and are thus attacked for being in league with Satan and unclean spirits – a not so dissimilar situation that greeted a newly created Christian religion who suffered bloody attacks from the ruling government in Rome.

Early Christians were thought to be necromancers and demon-worshipers. It was widely reported that they conducted secret ceremonies that involved infanticide, blood sacrifices and cannibalism. This smear campaign was so successful that a persecuted Christianity was forced to essentially remain a "secret society" for centuries – conducting their religious ceremonies in secret caves and tombs. A condition that did little to improve their already tattered image among the pagan population.

Later, this same campaign of accusing other religions of demon-worshiping along with distasteful ceremonies was eagerly used by the Church to reinforce their newly found dominance over the pagan religions. We can see this time honored tradition today as some religious writers express their viewpoint that UFOs and their occupants are actually demons under the guise of helpful space brothers.

A good example of the "Satan Flies the Saucers" belief can be found in the article *The Great Flying Saucer Myth* by Kelly G. Seagraves who writes: "What are these beings from outer space? I truly believe that we are being visited by beings that are extraterrestrial. I do not believe beings live on other planets. I believe that these visitors are fallen angels who have come to prepare the kingdom of the antichrist on this planet. I believe these are the same sons of God who came to have relationships with the daughters of men either physically or through some type of possession in Genesis 6, and produced a race of people who did not believe in the true God. I believe the same signs and wonders contributed to the great destruction in the past, and perhaps the men of renown who were born of fallen angels, the mighty men and giants described in Genesis 6, helped contribute to the unbelief of multitudes before the flood. I believe this explains why when God judged and destroyed the race in the great flood these giants and mighty men of renown were no more.

"I believe also that this fits with Peter's discussion Noah and the flood in his second epistle. The certain angels there said to be bound in the chains are those which participated in that terrible act of rebellion before the flood. They are chained and reserved unto judgment as a sign to others not to participate in the same disobedience. I believe this illustrates the fact that angels as revealed in the Bible, even fallen ones, have many powers, including the power of deception and others that we do not ordinarily attribute to them.

120

FLYING SAUCERS IN THE HOLY BIBLE

"Already Satanism is on the rise. The church of Satan worships openly, using the Satanic Bible. The belief in UFOs and aliens is simply another way in believing and worshiping Satan."

So is this belief true? Are UFOs and their occupants fallen angels who have taken on the guise of friendly space brothers – claiming to be here to help us, while actually after our immortal souls? Or is this merely disinformation from people fearful of different beliefs and religions, looking for ways to counteract the inevitable changes that take place as the centuries roll by?

The term flying saucer religion can be applied to a number of religious groups which invest alien contact with religious significance. Such contact is most often made on a psychic level with a member of an advanced alien race. Generally the benign aliens bring to the human race doctrine concerning spiritual advancement and eschatology. The beliefs of flying saucer religions are characteristically eclectic and often dove-tail eastern and western traditions. This ecumenical feat is accomplished by identifying historic religious figures such as Jesus Christ and the Buddha Gautama with advanced alien beings. The New Testament is a key eschatological influence for most of these new religious movements, and both premillennial and postmillennial groups exist.

Flying saucer religions are new religious movements born of a common American history. Similar to other religions in their infancy, these new religious movements are formed as one or two leaders attract a small following. The leaders of these religions, termed contactees, are those who have established a steady contact with their space brothers. Through these contactees, followers have access to spiritual instruction which in turn prepares them for their cosmic eschatological expectations. Replacing the role of contactee with that of a channeller results in a religious phenomenon analogous to spiritualism. This is no coincidence, since nearly all flying saucer religions are heavily influenced by Theosophy.

How are these new religious movements important?

Historians have classified American religions in two categories: mainstream and outsiders. Mainstream religions are those which have contributed the most to American religious history and usually claim the largest membership. Religious outsiders are those marginalized groups unable to gain complete acceptance into the mainline culture. Without doubt, flying saucer religions are outsiders in the religious market, although most of these groups have not been hotbeds for religious controversy. The obvious exception to this is the wide publicity given to the Heaven's Gate ritual suicide. This raises the following question: does controversy define an important moment in American history?

In 1878, the Mormon church, a definite religious outsider at the time, fought over the issue of polygamy in the landmark case of Reynolds v. U.S. The Supreme Court decided that U.S. citizens can believe anything, although citizens can not necessarily put their beliefs into practice. Religious outsiders can, despite being a minority, shape the religious atmosphere of the U.S. through controversy. The historian R. Laurence Moore stated, "If sustained controversy denotes cultural importance, then Mormons were as significant as any other religious group in nineteenth-century America." In this light, UFO religions, their origins, and their predecessors are relevant to modern religious history. These beliefs are of interest, because they reflect the more diverse manifestations of religious pluralism in the world.

Samuel Eaton Thompson was one of the first to take the flying saucer phenomenon to a new level. On March 28, 1950, Thompson claimed to have physically encountered and communicated with several Venusians in their spacecraft. While this encounter did not receive nation-wide publicity, Thompson's encounter closely resembles later contact phenomenon. The aliens told Thompson of the Second Coming of Christ in the year A.D. 10,000. These Venusians would arrive once again to enlighten the corrupt earthlings so that the path of Christ might be prepared. Such apocalyptic messages, whether premillennial or postmillennial, are a common feature of most contact accounts. The most influential of the early contactees was George Adamski, a California occultist. Adamski made physical contact with his first Venusian on November 20, 1952 in a California desert. Adamski later wrote several popular books which detailed his contact experiences and included drawings of aliens and spacecraft. Adamski's books borrowed heavily from the works of the Theosophist Madame Blavatsky. The Theosophical interpretation of alien contact is an approach used by most flying saucer religions.

Shortly after Adamski published his first book, many other contactees appeared on the scene. Some contactees communicated with aliens while in their physical presence, although most channeled messages from the aliens through telepathy or automatic writing. Possessing a steady contact with the alien entity, the channellers were the contactees most likely to gather a following.

The earliest influential flying saucer group was the **Heralds of the New Age** founded in the 1950s and located in New Zealand. It was Gloria Lee, backed by the Cosman Research Foundation, who really launched the extraterrestrial channeling movement in the U.S. Lee relayed the messages of J.W., an alien from Jupiter, through frequent newsletters and two highly Theosophical books titled *Why We are Here* and *The Changing Condition of Your World*.

Having received spacecraft construction plans from J.W., Lee traveled to Washington in 1962 so that she might present them to the U.S. government. Until she heard from the government, J.W. instructed Lee to fast while locked in a hotel room. After sixty-six days, Gloria Lee lapsed into a coma and died several days later. Gloria Lee's death was, however, far from insignificant. Many new flying saucer groups were inspired to organize shortly thereafter, and existing ones began to channel her spirit.

FLYING SAUCERS IN THE HOLY BIBLE

Why have UFOs and the belief in extraterrestrials' garnered so much interest and concern in this day and age? Strange, glowing objects flying about in the sky are nothing new as most surviving ancient writings will attest – so why should we now suddenly start paying attention to something that has been occurring apparently since the beginning of time?

Some Biblical scholars speculate that interest in UFOs is at an all time high because of what is referred to as "the end-time delusion." That "non-human" intelligence's, disguised as space people, are infiltrating our society with the intention of placing the "antichrist" in a position of world power sometime in the near future. This viewpoint is predominately embraced by fundamentalist Christian groups in the United States who eagerly look for any evidence that the end of the world will happen soon. These groups, certain of their own perfection over the rest of the world, have even gone as far as to fund terrorist operations in the U.S. and Israel in order to speed up the process of Armageddon.

One website that advocates the belief in Satanic UFOs glibly states: "The spiritual development of mankind has been guided by nonhuman intelligence's whose agenda has been to infiltrate, and even instigate, religious traditions in all cultures– and these nonhuman intelligence's are now pretending to be enlightening aliens. Legends of cultures ranging from Babylonian to Hindu to Native American are laden with beings who possess superior technology, spiritual beings enjoying worship and reverence in exchange for distributing wisdom."

Guy Malone in his book ***Come Sail Away: UFO Phenomenon & The Bible*** (1998 Seekye1.com), writes that any belief system other than the Bible is inherently Satanic in nature: "The true issue at hand here is not whether UFO and "visitor" happenings are real or not.I believe that they are. The issue is whether they really are extraterrestrial life forms, here to help us – or demons, with the express purpose of deceiving multitudes. Jesus said that we could recognize a tree by the fruit it bears (Matt 7:15, Sermon on the Mount) ... there are, all over the Bible, descriptions of demonic forces that have the specific task of "blinding the minds of unbelievers (2 Cor 4:4, earlier)" so that they will not be able to believe the gospel when it is preached to them... Almost all the books on UFOs are found in the New Age section of your local bookstore. Examine the fruit of the UFO culture. Does it lead people to Jesus? Do you know of any strong adherents to the UFO culture, who believe aliens are among us, that are also ... Bible-believing Christians? If you have a strong interest in UFOs, are you a Christian? Generally, those who have a strong faith in UFOs also have a non-Christian belief system that would be described as New Age."

What these writers fail to realize is that UFOs and UFO sightings enjoy a rich tradition in the Bible that was embraced by the writers and readers alike as evidence of Gods rich tapestry of creation. These Biblical miracles were not considered to be Satanic, but instead were seen as evidence of Gods true love for us and the ultimate mystery of life.

FLYING SAUCERS IN THE HOLY BIBLE

THE NEW MILLENNIUM RELIGION

I almost hate to use the term "New Millennium" since it has already been used to such excess that it has become cliched. However, it best describes what may be in store for future generations: A religion that uses a belief in space people as its divine emissaries. If you look back at the creation of all of the world's religions you will find striking similarities in their development and the growth and belief of UFOs and aliens.

All major religions generally start out as another religion's heresy. The Hebrew faith was a heresy from the earlier pagan religions, and Christianity was certainly considered a Jewish heresy. The new religions developed from the roots of the old, and they carried with them various doctrines of belief to insure their continued existence.

This process is propagated by the visionary experiences of prophets and their contacts with divine beings. These entities deliver messages of spiritual teachings and prophecies for the ever-growing faithful. This system occurs rapidly at first, but them tapers off to a slower but sustained growth that may take hundreds of years to fully develop. This is exactly what we have experienced this century with the UFO phenomena. The next several centuries will show whether the UFO religion will be able to sustain itself. Its disciples, due to their faith in friendly space people awaiting us in the cosmos, may be responsible for the scientific developments that will finally propel mankind off the planet and into the universe. Something that may be the ultimate goal of whatever is controlling the process.

The day will come when somewhere out in space mankind will finally run across another civilization. At that time we may ask them why they have been flying around in our skies all these years with their flying saucers. Their response could very well be: "Us? We thought it was you flying around our skies!"

High on a cathedral ceiling in Russia this mural is sure to puzzle most tourists who visit there, as it was painted hundreds of years before satellites were first launched in the former USSR.

124

FLYING SAUCERS IN THE HOLY BIBLE

ABOUT THIS BOOKS CONTRIBUTORS

Timothy Green Beckley is president Inner Light Publications and Global Communications, a publishing firm that specializes in controversial and "alternative topics." He is one of the nation's leading authorities on UFOs, and was even invited to speak to The House of Lords in England by his friend the late Earl of Clancarty, Brinsley Le Poer Trench. Beckley has appeared on hundreds of radio and TV talk shows and is the author of over fifteen books including *Psychic and UFO Revelations in the Last Days*, *The Secret Prophecy of Fatima Reveled*, and has edited over 25 nationally distributed publications such as *UFO Universe*, *Prophecy and Predictions*, *Conspiracies and Cover-Ups*.

Professor G. Cope Schellhorn was born in Sparta, Wisconsin and grew up in Kansas City, Missouri. He is a retired English professor who taught at the University of North Dakota, the University of Iowa and South Suburban College, Cook County, Illinois. Professor Schellhorn continues his research and writing and tends his orchard in Southwestern Wisconsin.

Sean Casteel resides in sunny California where he writes full time. He is a Contributing Editor of American UFO Magazine, and has written for such important publications as *Fate*, *UFO Universe*, *Angels and Aliens*, and *Conspiracies and Coverups*. His first book titled *Nikola Tesla Journey to Mars: Are We Already There?* was recently released by Global Communications.

Tim Swartz is a television producer and a five-time Emmy winner who lives in Jasper, Indiana. Swartz has traveled the globe researching and investigating UFOs and paranormal phenomena. Using his background in television journalism, Swartz has written numerous articles for such well-known publications as *Strange Magazine*, *UFO Universe*, *Unsolved UFO Sightings*, *Uncensored UFO Reports*, *Shadowmag*, *Atlantis Rising*, and *Conspiracies and Coverups*. He has also authored a number of critically acclaimed books such as *The Lost Journals of Nikola Tesla*, *Teleportation: From Star Trek to Tesla*, and *Time Travel: A How-To Insiders Guide*, co-authored with Commander X.

Dr. Virginia F. Brasington (now deceased) was a foremost authority on Biblical text, in particular the New Testament. She was licensed as a minister in the State of North Carolina by the Church of the Nazarene. Her book Flying Saucers in the Bible was originally published in the 1960's by Gray Barkers Saucerian Publications and later reprinted by permission of the original publisher as well as the estate of the author.